The
FACE
of
EXPRESSION

Aaron Woodson

authorHOUSE°

AuthorHouse™
1663 Liberty Drive
Bloomington, IN 47403
www.authorhouse.com
Phone: 1 (800) 839-8640

Published by AuthorHouse 01/31/2018

ISBN: 978-1-5462-2261-3 (sc)
ISBN: 978-1-5462-2793-9 (e)

Print information available on the last page.

BEAUTIFUL STRUGGLE

By Aaron Woodson

Ever since birth, I've had to endure a beautiful struggle. My mother strained every last ounce of energy during labor for me to arrive. As I grew, it became a struggle for me to take my first steps. I stumbled and fell a few times, but I kept getting up and trying again. My lips would quiver and hesitate to speak its first words. Although I stuttered, I somehow managed to get my point across. My little hands were quite slippery as I tried to catch or grab hold of something. Often times I struggled to listen as a result of my short attention span. While going to school, I struggled to complete my homework when it was due. And how could I forget the nights I struggled out of bed to get to the bathroom? Waking up early for work was my least favorite thing to do. Oh, how I struggled! I've always dreamed of romance, but it never mixed with the expense of finance. As I got a little older, I struggled with my approach to the opposite sex. It was embarrassing when I struggled for my first time! My enthusiasm lacked stimulation, like having no erection. Enduring sacrifice overshadowed my happiness like a dark cloud covering the sun. When I became mature, I gained wisdom through each trial and tribulation. I'm a stranger here on earth, but I'm related to the struggle like it was my brother. However, all I was searching for was a father and I found him in Jesus Christ. Through realization, I came to the conclusion that it wasn't easy to walk with Jesus. I struggled w/ my faith as if I was balancing on a tight rope and He was with me all the way through.

Your struggle and my struggle look at each other in the same mirror; it reflects how beautiful our struggle really is!

MAN IN THE MIRROR

By Aaron Woodson

When I step forward and take a look at myself in the mirror, I see a boy who has fully grown into a man. "When I was a child I thought and spoke as a child, but when I became a man I put away those childish things." This man I see in the mirror is looking back at me as if to challenge me to make a difference. I look deep within and ask my heart, do I really have what it takes to make a change? In the wears of my eyes, tears fill up and trickle down my dark cheeks like a waterfall. No longer can I be blind to what's happening around me...I'm tired of seeing a world tortured with suffering, poverty, and depression. Starting here and now with the man in the mirror, I'm leaving a lasting impression that gives everyone a chance to wake up with a smile. I'm looking at my reflection with brand new eyes, with a new walk, a new talk, and a new attitude. Do I like what I see? There are some things that I'm not proud of, but I've come a long way. I'm not what I used to be and each day I live I become more satisfied with who I am... the man in the mirror!

WHAT **I** WORK FOR

By Aaron Woodson

Most people spend their lives working to adapt in these
times. People work to survive and carry the load because
no one else will. There are no other alternatives. People
work because they have choices but they are limited.
They are either poor and rely on economic security to
make their living or they work hard and live to make
ends meet or to live the dream. Some people work
tirelessly and diligently, yet sometimes they never get
to enjoy the fruits of their labor. They just deal with
the spoilage of the fruit that tastes rotten, and it seems
like that is all that is left for them. Making life easy
is like trying to make lemons into lemonade. Trying
to seek the shade for refuge, but there is no escape
from the burdens of everyday life. The rewards for
the fruits of labor are next to nothing and goes to the
salaries of the rich. All we seem to get is crumbs off
the table...everything else is swept under the carpet.
When the smoke clears and the dust settles, the only
thing we work for is to live another day. All we are is
just a number in the system, something we all have in
common which is Social Security. Politicians campaign
and try to persuade us to vote for them. Claiming

they will make our lives "better" and making empty promises they have no intentions of fulfilling. When they get elected the only thing we have to look forward to is paying taxes and losing our jobs. Whatever happened to the American Dream? I'm sure we're all pretty familiar with it; the big house with a white picket fence, big family, and a nice car. Do you know we're still waiting to get those 40 acres of land and a mule? We understand we have to work even though most of hate our jobs, but where are the ends that justify the means? It's like a rat race, everyone is fighting over one little piece of cheese. Everybody wants a piece of the pie, but the problem is we are fighting over scraps which add to our frustration. Work is inevitable in our future... not retirement! Even if we live long enough to see our retirement, the countdown begins for when we meet our expiration date. What do we have to look forward to honestly? You be the judge. And who do we really work for? We work for the federal government courtesy of the U.S.A.

FILLING THE SHOES

By Aaron Woodson

Shoes are meant to be worn, but most of us aren't born to fit them. Most of us try to fill someone else's shoes, but need to be more concerned with their own size. Some are blessed to walk through life as if it were a breeze. For others, it's more like stumbling upon a tree stump. There are times we'll get a few lumps and bumps from running into walls or falling down on the asphalt. Bruises and scars remind us of what endeavors we've encountered through time. Shoes welcome our feet and sometimes we wear it out like we were in a marathon. Sometimes shoes are filled with sand, it gradually starts to slow us down. Blisters and calluses take form when things rub us the wrong way. Remember that it takes endurance to get through the trials and tribulations of life. Take your place in your own race and go at your pace. Only one person can fill your shoes...YOU!

Stress Addict

By Aaron Woodson

Some people sell, buy, and abuse drugs...in their
possession is a substance. It's used for the purpose it's
intended...to get you addicted. If there is one thing that
is like a drug, it would be stress! Most of us are stress
addicts...our lives are conflicted with jealousy, anger,
financial debt, drama, pressure, and among other
things. If we keep going like this, we'll be sure to
overdose over all this stress! Like a closet in disarray,
we clutter so many unnecessary things that we don't
need in our lives. Sometimes we dress up in our stress
clothes...looking worn down and beat up! Smoking our
cancer, thinking we getting high...but we only increase
the chances of disease. We can all die any day and we
can die from anything. But what kills us the most ladies
and gentlemen, is stress! Do you want to be responsible
giving birth to a generation of stress? I don't think
you do, so you need to stop being a stress addict
and go to relieve yourself from it. Your therapy will
help you cope as long as quit doping your mind with
constant stress! From a stress addict to another, let's seek
out a healthier resolution and be at peace with ourselves
and our situations.

NUMB IT DOWN FOR YOU

By Aaron Woodson

Attention everybody, school is in session. This is no time for recess! Things have changed and now we must learn a new curriculum. Back and forth like a pendulum, we've been hit hard with tough times. A message of hope persuades us to open our ear drums... now we anxiously await a new era. For too long we have been under the thumb of political tyranny. Paying our dues, yet we still sing the blues. Eyes are glued to the television for the evening news...yet our vision is blurred from all the sketchy details. Media and radio control the airwaves...however the message doesn't come in so loud and clear. Living in a world of fear, it's a wonder why people shed so many tears. The clock is ticking and people keep taking a licking...how much more can we endure? If we keep going like this, might as well numb us with Novocain so we can deal with all this pain. That's how we numb it down for you!

99.9%

By Aaron Woodson

How close are you to perfection? Most people would say they are close to it, while some others would say they aren't even close. There are few that seem so sure they have reached that hallmark. I'm not perfect by any means, but I will tell you that I've mastered the art of just being me. I only make up .01% of the population... so what makes me stand out from the rest of the 99.9%? My uniqueness and personality separate me from the rest of the pack. Striving for perfection, yet looking past my reflection...I only see ordinary! Is 99.9% just only ordinary? Maybe. 100% is flawless, in other words extraordinary. 99.9% is so close, yet it means nothing. The way I see it, 99.9% doesn't meet some people's expectations. Trying to make it a priority to reach superiority...however I just fall short! Is it fair to judge anything less than 100% as mediocrity? Sometimes we forget that we have limitations and that we are human. No excuses, just facts of life. There is always room for improvement, but there is usually a replacement not too far behind. I know I'm 99.9% better than any man that claims he can try to take you from me. They can try, but I guarantee you that they will fail 99.9% of the time. Sometimes it may seem like we argue 99.9% of the time, but we always work things out for the best. If I gave you everything you asked for 99.9% of the time, would you take it for granted? If you gave me everything I asked for 99.9% of the time, would I take you for granted? Of course not, because I appreciate everything you do for me. If I told you the truth 99.9% of the time would you doubt me? If I told you a lie 99.9% of the time would you think it's the truth? I've told some lies and many truths in my lifetime. I admit 99.9% of the time that I've make mistakes...but make no mistake, I love you with everything that I am. No one else comes close. When I look in those beautiful eyes of yours, I see forever you and me. I'm your one and only...the rest of me is whole because I'm with the woman of my dreams 99.9% of the time...Tatum!

POETRY THAT BLEEDS FROM MY PEN

By Aaron Woodson

The entrance is open for all to witness the drama...the passion...the art...which is known as my poetry! After my performance, I will make my own grand finale and bow out like the graceful entertainer that I am. Without further a due, let me introduce to you the poetry that bleeds from my pen. I write swiftly with each stroke of the pen...I leave my mark, better known as my trademark swagger. I cut into my adversaries like a dagger and leave scars all over their conscience. Their pain is splattered all over...it's all over when I write their wrongs and pass the bill to the judicial system. Send them to the pen and put em' on lock down! I've been there before and ain't no bars ever gonna hold me now! Jesus was buried in a tomb w/ a stone covering his final resting place. On the third day he was resurrected and became a Rolling Stone! He is my inspiration and He blessed me with the gift of poetry. It's like floetry in motion...taking it to the next level. I refuse to fold like origami paper...I'm too bold and too cold to be outlasted in this showcase of wits! I am fit to wear the crown...and to all my haters that have a frown, let me just say...hi, hater! I'm rewriting history and you can put me in the Guinness world record books...cuz I'm breaking trends and making headlines. Got you all seeing stars and now you're in the midst of a superstar. What bleeds from my pen will put you in a state of shock. What bleeds from my pen will put you on ice. What bleeds from my pen will make your liver quiver. What bleeds from my pen will make you shiver. The poetry that bleeds from my pen will deliver my thoughts...my struggles...my pain...my joy...etc. The poetry that bleeds from my pen will serve as a reminder of whose next in line. Don't get out of line now because I'm going to put you in your place. The poetry that bleeds from my pen expresses my admission of guilt, but also my innocence. And the poetry that bleeds from the pen is the man writing from his heart and soul...Mr. Aaron T. Woodson!

THE AUTHOR OF MY LIFE

By Aaron Woodson

I came out the womb butt naked and experienced
my first few breaths of fresh air. To be certain that I
exist, I have my very own birth certificate. My arrival
into this life was made possible by God, the author of
my life! He has written every chapter that I'm living
and He will also write the last. A beginning is like a
sunrise, you barely make it over the horizon...An ending
is like a sunset, you go down to signal your retirement.
I will someday fulfill all my requirements to this life of
mine and meet my expiration date. For now I'm just
enjoying my date with destiny and there will be a few
times I may flirt with death. But until that happens, I
will live out the rest of my days with the love I bear in
my heart. You can hand me a death certificate now or
later...but I'm still a vessel that has wind blowing in its
sails. When the wind stops, then I will sink like the
titanic and go down in history! Happily ever after and
thereafter...in heaven is where I ascend to be, with the
author of my life!

I REMEMBER

By Aaron Woodson

I'm in living color at this moment and now I slowly fade to black and white. My crystal ball reveals my life as if I were looking at my own reflection in the past, present, and future. I have no memory of being an embryo in my mother's womb. I only remember how I was brought into this world. I remember my first words...as I'm sure to remember my last. I remember when I learned to crawl. And how can I forget taking my first baby steps? I remember listening to the sound of my mother's voice that comforted me. I remember when I used to cry and yes, I even cry to this day. I remember when I was sick and how she took care of me. I remember when I was in pain. I remember when it would rain. I remember how I laughed...I remember how I danced around the house....and did I mention that I remember singing in the shower? Funny, how I remember playing games like hide and seek when I was a child. But now, I'm a man and I've put those childish things away. I remember what I was taught...I remember where I started and where I came from. I remember when I grew up without a father. I remember when my family used to be so close. I remember the heart to heart talks I had with my family. I remember the times I'd ask for help. I remember when I felt like giving up. I remember the friendships I made throughout my lifetime. I remember losing a few friends. I remember losing the ones I loved. I even remember when I first fell in love. I remember when I fell out of love. How can I not remember my first kiss? Oh, how sweet it was! I remember my "first time" like it was my last time. I remember my proudest moment. I remember my darkest hour. I remember how lonely I felt at times. I remember how happy I used to be when you came around. I remember the day I said "I love you." I remember when I looked into your eyes. I remember how much I meant to you. I remember how much you meant to me. I remember what we shared between us. I will always remember these things for all times...just remember that no matter what, I will remember you for the rest of my life.

WHAT RUNS DEEP

By Aaron Woodson

In the middle of open water, as I fight to stay afloat...I realize what really runs deep. Nothing can go beyond the depth of blood and every time I've shed my outpour, it ran deeper than the Red Sea. I've parted ways with some people, maybe it's because some of those people changed. Or perhaps I outgrew the ones I cared for or even loved. No one is to blame, because things never remain the same. Been to many places where I have taken names and saw many faces. Out with the old and in with the new. It's just that easy to be replaced. Memories are good to reflect on sometimes, but I'm way past all of that now. Growing up made me open my eyes. Reality set in and the truth set me free. Every man and woman bleeds...some of them bleed to show their vulnerability. Some bleed for sacrifice. I've bled internally and externally many times over and it sure won't be the first or last time. If you can find my vein then you would really know what runs deep!

Cleanin' up my act

By Aaron Woodson

Gazing into my closet, I see a dark and cluttered scene. I begin to reminisce of what life was like before I got myself into this mess. Realizing I must dismiss the notion of regret, I take some aspirin to relieve myself of my troubling thoughts. A pile of dirty clothes catches attention. Within an instant, I know that perhaps I should do some laundry. I don't like to air out my dirty laundry or anyone elses for that matter, however I'm happy to put it in the washer at anytime. Much like a washer and dryer, we go through our cycles in life. Wash, rinse, spin, and dry! Much like our clothes, we all need to iron out those wrinkles we have once in awhile. Unfortunately we can't take out the ones that are visible on our faces because those come with age. Yet we can still wash our face and body everyday. Should you not wash the inside as you would the outside? Clean on the inside, clean on the outside...nice of you all to clean up your act! I'm not exempt, so don't tempt me to do any dirt because I too am cleanin' up my act!

LABOR

By Aaron Woodson

Uh oh...something has just happened! Wait a second; my wife's water just broke. With a sense of urgency, I swiftly rush her to the emergency room as she is officially in labor. The expression on her face details the excruciating pain that she is enduring. Reminds me of a familiar episode I've watched so many times before. Blood, sweat, and tears usher in an era of constant sacrifice. Labor is our way of life, just ask Adam and Eve about it. We should count our blessings daily because without labor, there wouldn't be any harvest! Through labor, we reap the benefits of what we sew. Time and money are spent through labor. Nothing would ever exist, if not for labor coming to the rescue. We owe labor a debt of gratitude for serving us the way it has for so long. We don't need to have a bad attitude against labor...it's necessary and besides there is a purpose for it! We don't need a holiday to relieve us from everyday labor...take time out for yourselves throughout each day and reflect on what labor has done for you lately.

DETERMINATION

By Aaron Woodson

Adrenaline is pumped inside my veins like gasoline. Meditation begins my determination to go where I've never been before. Sweat drips out of my pores to form an ocean as I sail to shore. Reaching higher ground, the sound of urgency echoes throughout the air. No matter the distance...no matter the weight...no matter the time...no matter my limitations, I will rise above the mountains and stars! Determination is the wind beneath my wings as I elevate straight to heaven.

RESILIENT

By Aaron Woodson

There is a word that comes to mind that is stuck somewhere between brilliant and valiant. I'm very familiar with her name and I've always known her to be resilient! We met at a place called rock bottom as my heart had eroded from a terrible break up! Stones were thrown and mudslides made things slippery...yet my feet still remained on solid ground. I found out that no matter what obstacle, distraction, or opposition I face...I know I will have a breakthrough! It's apparent that I've been through some emotional turmoil yet I'm ready to bury the hatchet and move forward with my life. Crawling back to the surface, I reach for the hand of God so that I won't fall into enemy territory. I stand tall because I have been delivered. Through leaps and bounds, mountains and valleys, ponds and oceans...I can truly say that I was resilient through it all.

MANNEQUIN

By Aaron Woodson

Strolling past the entrance into the mall, bright lights illuminate throughout the building. Magic is in the air and I see beautiful women w/ long hair walking' by my way! Like a penguin, I'm waddling' in pursuit and keep a cool demeanor. A nearby mannequin catches my eye and I stop chasing my pipe dream. Elegantly sculptured from head to toe, I begin to contemplate what it would be like to go on a date with her. A guy like me could surely show this mannequin a real good time. I could be her chauffeur and take her out to a night on the town. Don't laugh at the idea, just go ahead and keep looking for those other fish in the sea. I have all I want and need from a mannequin to call my very own.

What It Means to Love Someone

By Aaron Woodson

When you hear the word love, what does it say to you?
Now listen carefully for the sound of it's pulse. It echoes
the sweetness that pours out from our ears like honey.
Love is an essential part of our daily nutrition in life.
Without it, we surely wouldn't survive. Like the endless
supply of air that we breathe, we all thrive on the
power of love. The creator of heaven and earth loved us
so much, that He gave His first and last breath for us so
that we could have everlasting life. He died on a cross
so that we all may have salvation. We meant so much to
Him that we He paid the ultimate price. Although we
are sinners, through his eyes he loves us unconditionally.
So what does it mean to love someone? Take a moment
to pay attention and you can see that we have the
perfect example to follow. Give willingly of yourself to
someone you truly love. There is no profit to gain from
love, just only the serviceable act of charity...and that
everyone is what it means to love someone!

REJECTION

By Aaron Woodson

Every time when it seems like I try to attempt a shot, somehow I always get rejected. Where can I go to find sanctuary from constant rejection? Perhaps I can retreat into isolated territory and conceal my pain from all this rain. I lay the burdens of my heart upon the altar and call on the name of God to get me through these changing weather patterns! I could never predict a forecast of rejection, however there is always a chance that it could happen and it did. Lately it has been so cold and on the evening news I've been told, I should expect to see a warm front arrive by morning! I know that I will find my neighbors company to be harmonious and together we rejoice. I will join them and sing a brand new song...it will be a song you will play over and over again and again and again! Don't rewind back to rejection, as we will now fast forward to acceptance! Push play and let your ears be mesmerized by this wonderful selection of Love and Happiness!

What Happened?

By Aaron Woodson

What seems like an eternity is only a year. What seems like a century is only a month. What seems like a year is only a few hours. And what seems like a few hours is only a few minutes. Everyone sells their time daily, yet they can't even buy a second back. What happened?

You happened!

When everything or everyone had passed me by, you were the one that made my heart stop in time. Your sweet voice echoed a chiming melody unto my ears. Every time you came near, tears of joy and excitement would form in the wears of my eyes. Now all I can do is sit here and reminisce about the promise of what would have been. So, I ask to myself...What happened?

DOUBLE LIFE

By Aaron Woodson

As I step out into the spotlight, the show begins and
I turn in a performance of a lifetime. Absorbing the
praise just like a sponge, I proceed to make my exit
from the stage. I start to drip and the evidence leaks
out what I've been desperately trying to hide. I want to
put the past behind me just like my shadow, however
it seems to follow my every move. Even though I walk
in the shadow of death, I will fear no evil. I walk a
fine line between right and wrong, trying to keep my
balance so I can still have a fighting chance. With
a flip of a coin, I have my good and bad sides. They
both fight against each other as one tries to prevail and
conquer the other. Armed with double-edged swords,
they swiftly attack to witness the drawing of first
blood! Back and forth we go and the stakes are high.
Double or nothing, I bet my life to allow someone else
to have a better one. I'm already in trouble and I'm just
now finding a way out of it...through salvation! No
longer in jeopardy from my life of crimes because
I stopped committing fouls and double dribbling...I
took a time out and listened to my coach, Jesus Christ!

DIAMONDS ARE NOT FOREVER

By Aaron Woodson

Everything that glitters isn't gold and everything
that shines doesn't make it a diamond. You took my
kindness for blindness and robbed my heart of a
treasure known as love. If I could measure my pain,
it would go beyond miles. When we first met, you
sparkled before my very eyes. I cherished and adored
you as if you were too good to ignore. The allure is
gone and now I've been lured into a deep depression.
Diamonds are precious to hold onto when you
understand their worth. We sometimes often treat
the ones we love like fiber glass rather than the rare
diamond we have in our possession. Diamonds can
be misplaced or misused if they are in the wrong
hands. Diamonds are tangible, yet we find it so hard to
let them go. Just because you give someone a diamond
doesn't make that person yours in the first place. Sure,
diamonds capture the imagination that begins with
our fascination...but they are not meant to win hearts
entirely. We have diamonds here on earth, yet eternally
they will no longer be in existence...God is forever,
diamonds are not!

ROAD TO MATURITY

By Aaron Woodson

As I prepare for the long haul to go onto the road of
maturity; I see signs showing me which direction to
take. I'm aware of the location the detours and dead
ends meet. Deciding to proceed with caution in the
intersection of transition; I come across the lonely road
of faith. As I drive on the straight and narrow, I feel as
though I will get bumped off by so many distractions.
However, as I begin to have control over my conscience,
I realize I was heading down the path of disillusion.
By grace, I'm able to progress towards my objective.
Excuse me for being so protective, just trying to counter
the obstacles of adversity. I didn't have to make it this
far to attend a university. Not an issue of immaturity,
just daydreaming about bathing in purity. As I speed
through the overpass of hope, the light of wisdom
illuminates my arrival to the road of maturity.

EXISTENCE

By Aaron Woodson

Head first, eyes wide open...life just begins for an infant
as if it were taking its first peek above the soil. A brand
new gift is given to the world to cherish; as parents,
as guardians, as mentors, and as disciplinarians...we
have a responsibility to raise our children in a loving
community that gives them a solid foundation for their
advancement. Children give us hope and they're the
future. The DNA was the blueprint and the autopsy will
be the end result. From the womb, an embryo is made.
The cycle continues like an assembly line. Children
multiply like a pandemic; however they all cure our
suffering world with the nature of their existence.

PARENTAL CONSENT

By Aaron Woodson

Sometimes parents just don't understand...too often they forget what it was like to be a kid or even being an adult that is quite capable of making their own decisions. They are like visionaries stuck in another time zone...their children are not living up to certain expectations. Nothing is ever good enough to give them the craving for their satisfaction.

Sometimes parents can become a distraction and you always find them in the equation. You don't need permission to receive a free admission to enjoy your life...however, we all need to honor our mother and father regardless if we have differences with either of them. Parents should not be an afterthought; after all they were the ones whom brought us into this world! We never had consent to be here, so why do we need parental consent to live the way we intend to for the rest of our lives?

SUICIDAL ROMANCE

By Aaron Woodson

Time is drawing close and it seems what we've shared is fleeting away. Gestures, threats, and actions have been well documented on the memo of my heart. Portraits and writings on the wall appear 3-D, but I've always been one-dimensional. What was once sensational is now confrontational. Our love has become suicidal and it feels as if we were victims of a homicide.
Trying to hide from all the recklessness, but no one emerges from this terrible wreck. Nothing was ever promised or guaranteed to begin with, we were just simply careless and heartless. My lips become speechless in this tragedy. Our meaningless romance committed suicide because we didn't put our love first. The lesson we've learned from this is everything fails without love. We auditioned to play a significant role in each other's lives…but now we lower the curtain to signal the inevitable…a suicidal romance gone bad!

THE LOVE TAX

By Aaron Woodson

What if there was a tax on love? Love is free, but it has to be earned. Just like how we have to earn our paychecks and acquire things that justify or satisfy our needs...we must earn the love we so richly desire. Every purchase comes with a tax, but God paid everyone's taxes by dying on a cross. We have to pay taxes for everything we use or consume. We assume that we are entitled to certain things, but nothing here belongs to us. Some of us make false claims that leave us in a debt of jeopardy! Love comes with pain and sacrifice. Taxes are subtracted from our incomes that are paid to the federal government. Like victims of a bank robbery, we see our wages paying the lucrative salaries of the rich! Will a man rob God? We owe God, not the IRS; the offering of a love tax for the repentance of our sins!

DEMOLITION MAN

By Aaron Woodson

What God has set out to create, man has set out to
destroy! That is why God is mindful of man. Made in
God's image and likeness, man was given dominion
over the earth by the creator. However, since man's
existence things have taken a downward spiral. Man has
achieved abundantly, yet there is a redundant defiance
of giving obedience to his master. Man is the student,
God is the teacher...men like to appear godly and yet
they are weak! Men have much to learn but have a
tendency to lean on their own understanding. Men have
the knowledge of good and evil; temptation brings forth
an appealing sabotage and men fall for its trap! Pride
goes before a fall...men have given birth to destruction
and turned away from instruction. Construction fails
without the right foundation and the architecture will
collapse at the hands of the demolition man!

Gentleman

By Aaron Woodson

I'm a gentleman...originated from man and woman.
Masculinity and feminism wrapped together all in one
like DNA. Holding' down my position like a CEO,
I stay on top looking for a TKO! Sharp as a tack, yet
genuine like fine wine. Cinnamon is my ingredient for
success; just a sprinkle and I'll always be sweet. The
words that slip off my tongue melt like butter on toast.
My walk glides like a cool summer breeze and my scent
makes every woman freeze. Wherever I go I make
everyone sneeze. Guess I didn't know people could be
allergic to a gentleman's swag!

MUSIC IS WHAT I KNOW

By Aaron Woodson

The countdown begins with your favorite host with the
most, Mr DJ.
As I check my crowd, I feel its pulse. The reception is
deafening, as they came to receive the blessing of music.

For years, we have all been one nation under a groove.
Music has given
birth to you and I alike. With its own identity, music
plays like an instrument as everything
flows N' Sync. Timeless as love and happiness, music is
encoded in our DNA...it's just simply built to last.

Whether it's past, present, or future...the music lives on
like a memory that's cherished forever. Oh, how music is
my latest, greatest inspiration. I keep fallin in love with
you. When I'm between the sheets, you're my comforter.
As I'm in the shower,
I contemplate about your sexual healing. I'm ready to
face you like the man in the mirror.

Sometimes I may have differences with you when it
comes to make-ups and break-ups, but I will always love

you no matter what. You're all that I have to confide in and this is why I know you so intimately. You're like my best friend...it's so incredible that you're unforgettable. This music is what I know!

WORDS

By Aaron Woodson

What we see triggers a thought...this begins a pattern
and starts a cycle like a washing machine. We absorb
thoughts like a sponge and it feeds us a hearty meal of
words! What we speak from our tongues is either life or
death. However, it's what we keep under our own breath
that is like lava waiting to erupt. Don't mean to be so
abrupt, just seeing what's corrupt! Words do hurt and
they are like swords that pierce through the soul. We've
become so bold that our words transform into action.
Our actions pave the way for reactions and sometimes
we get lost in all these distractions. Where do we go to
see the latest attraction? "Oh, I know! We can go to the
zoo of habits and see how they're put into practice. We
learn and adapt to our surroundings, everything else
becomes second nature. We are mature creatures aren't
we? And now it's time to showcase what we've mastered
and put it into our character.

SHATTERED

By Aaron Woodson

Somewhere hearts have been broken; lives left
shattered in pieces. Everything appears to have
fallen apart. We're scattered among the earth like a
puzzle. Some of us don't know where we fit. Most
of us know that something is missing. Images are
distorted like a kaleidoscope; where can we go to
find clarity? Sometimes there is nothing left to do
but scream. Trying to enjoy a good night's rest, but I
wake up feeling battered by unknown assailants. All
that mattered has now been left shattered.

COSMETIC UNIVERSE

By Aaron Woodson

Before there was make up, there was just simply the natural. Woman was made from man and made into his counterpart. After creation some things began to fall apart. Woman was beautifully and wonderfully crafted to be a masterpiece of art. Woman isn't just ordinary, she is extraordinary and phenomenal! She is like a mirror that shows man his own heart's reflection. The pain she endures cuts like a knife and yet she still bleeds nothing but constant affection. So, for her protection, she conceals what lies beneath with artificial cosmetics. She carries around baggage of pollutants, thinking she needs a make-over. Silly girl, you're just fine the way you are. There are plenty of gentlemen that adore you and could never ignore a goddess in their midst. Women are the center of their man's universe; that's why we are so drawn to you in the first place. The symmetry you possess begins our chemistry. Honey, you're an industry all by yourself and that's all you need to advertise! You're every man's favorite commercial and we see you for more than this cosmetic universe!

LOVE'S TRANSLATION

By Aaron Woodson

We all know that love is its own origin and it dwells in every corner of the world. People may be different outwardly, but they all share the common need and assurance of love. We learn to speak and indentify with our own special language that defines who we are. Love speaks to all of us and there is no language barrier. Love transcends beyond our expectations and descends upon the world like the fall of rain. Love is like a runaway train, once it picks up steam there is just no stopping it! It covers its tracks and travels an unknown distance. For instance, love is not part of any curriculum...it's a pendulum that goes back and forth. Love isn't bilingual, it's universal...remember that the translation comes from our own heart's interpretation.

If I COULD GIVE

By Aaron Woodson

If I could give you anything, I would give you the very thing that beats in my chest. I will not rest until I give you the best. If I could give you anything, I'd give you plenty of showers that would last for hours. If I had the power to change the weather, I'd make it snow and be your leather coat to keep you warm at night. If you were blind, I'd give you my eyes to have better sight. If you were short on height, I'd stand tall for you like a tower. If I could, I would give you an island that was named after you. Even that wouldn't be enough because you are like your own continent. If I could, I would give you the world and everything that surrounds it. If I could, I would give you my life so you could have a better one. If I can help it, I'd give you my promise to always be your one and only and never leave you lonely. If only you knew, what I'd give to just be with you.

JUST NOT CUT OUT FOR THIS

By Aaron Woodson

Follow the dotted line...oops; I just cut outside the line. How can I repair the damage? I try to fix the mistake I've made, but yet it doesn't make everything better! I can move on and hope to not make the same mistake twice, but I just can't seem to get it right the first time. I'm just not cut out for this! Whatever I touch, leads to disaster. Whatever I say digs me a hole that I can never seem to get out of. Whatever I do makes me look and feel stupid sometimes. Most of you may wonder why are you so hard on yourself. Because I'm my own worst critic. When I think people laugh with me, they are actually laughing at me. Who am I kidding? Seems like I'm not cut out for anything...not even you! I don't deserve you because I seem to push you away further. I would feel naked without you in my life...now I'm left out in the cold. I'm shiver all over and the nights get lonelier when you're not around. I miss you so much, but I just didn't make the cut when it matter most.

STOLE ME AWAY

By Aaron Woodson

I remember just like it was yesterday. One day you came into my life like a thief in the night and stole me away. You broke in and entered my heart...then you robbed me of all my love. You took the most valuable thing to me and I had no choice but to surrender it to you. I ask myself, is it truly a crime to take someone's love? I guess if it's there for the taking, and then seize it. It's not every day you have an opportunity to get what you want. Baby, you have me in your possession...so, now that you have me, what are you going to do with me? You can tie me up, lock me up, and throw away the key...whatever, just as long as you plead your case with a helpful demonstration! ;) Let's leave all the evidence behind... you got me all caught up in the first place, so c'mon and let's get caught in the act. When you're done with me just make sure you put me back where you found me. I can't believe you stole me away. Hmmm.

I Tried

By Aaron Woodson

All these years, I've tried to be all I could ever be...the best I could be. I tried to be there for you...I tried to be your shelter...I tried to be your sunshine...I tried to make things right between us. I tried to understand where we went wrong. Sadly, I have no answer for these efforts. I tried to stay when I should have left. Sometimes I tried to walk away from it all. I tried to give you my all. I tried with all of my heart. I cried with all of my heart. And I died trying...I lived trying... just wasn't quite good enough. I'm thankful for my existence...but in my last sentence, just remember that I tried!

SOMEONE IN THE DARK

By Aaron Woodson

Come out, come out wherever you are. I know you're there...For quite some time now, you've been lurking in the shadows trying to get under my skin. You're more like a thorn in my side and now there is nowhere to run or hide. What's done in the dark must come to the light eventually...finally I can expose you for the villain that you are. Come face to face with your worst nightmare...I will give you something to really be afraid of! You try and try to take what is mine, but you never can prevail and you fail miserably. You attempt to hold a cloud of jealousy over my head...but instead I pour down my furious vengeance upon you. I will strike you down like a lightning bolt...and you will find yourself in my path of destruction. Listen carefully to my instructions...don't come around here making it known that you're an intruder. Stay in your own backyard, cuz if you don't I will bury you! This isn't for the weak at heart nor is it a walk in the park...just someone in the dark that now has become the hunted. Beware!

FRENEMY

By Aaron Woodson

Friends...how many of us have them? How many can we depend on? I use to consider you a close friend, but you no longer have that title. You lost it when you decided to betray me and throw dirt in my eye. You did the crime and I became the victim through guilt by association. I've endured the pain of losing a friendship...the hurtful deeds still play like flashbacks. I study them over and over in my mind, thinking how I can seek retribution. But then again, I'm not like you and I never will be like you. You took my kindness for weakness... now all that is left is bittersweet! Broken silence breaks the ice...now you pay the price and be left out in the cold. You sold me with your cheap imitation and finally I'm giving you my best retaliation...I'm offering to only be your frenemy. I'll be the best frenemy you ever had!

MAKE WAR OR MAKE BABIES

By Aaron Woodson

Bombs away, let the bodies hit the floor...everything
blasted to smithereens'! What's going on? Lord, have
mercy! Why make war, when you can make babies!
From baby boomers to today's generation, we all live
and experience the art of war! Nothing pretty about it,
just a gory tale of senseless brutality! It's been said that
bad boys move in silence, never in violence! However
that's not always true...there is always a mess that gets
left behind. Someone has to clean it up just like 9-11. As
God as my witness, let me speak my peace and pledge
my allegiance to life after death! If I l die anytime before
today's end and tomorrow's beginning... I know I have
something to carry on my legacy...to carry on my name!
Let the walls of Jericho fall by the tune of trumpets
harmony and welcome the birth of a spawning new
generation. Music makes babies and brings hope...war
deprives us these inspiring things! Home, sweet home...
baby; don't wait up for me I'll be back before you know
it! I love you.

DOWN 2 A T!

By Aaron Woodson

Dedicated to Tatum

The chemistry between us is unlike anything I've ever experienced before. I feel like I have this down to a science...Down 2 a T! It's a true pleasure and honor to have you by my side. No longer could I hide what I feel in this little heart of mine. Whenever you're in close proximity, my love for you explodes like dynamite. The wind blew you in my direction and our predicted forecast has been nothing short of an emotional high! Let's ride on the rollercoaster of love and break the speed and sound barrier. You hit me like a tidal wave that I never saw coming. The force rushed through me like a hard tackle. I tried to defend my heart, but you managed to score a winning touchdown somehow. Seems like the last play came Down 2 a T! Like a referee, what we have between us is official! There won't be any flags for any unnecessary roughness or holding...because we can let things slide once we make it to another arena... the bedroom! Anything goes and we have our own rules that we follow. Baby, I can't get enough of you...

your scent drives me wild...your body talks to me... and your words soothe me like a therapy session. There won't be any recession, just a lesson in the signs of love making. My greatest inspiration is you...you're all I've ever desired in a woman. I will be gentle, experimental, instrumental, and a little sentimental. Only because I love you and I always will. I came up short on a few plays in the past, but now I've made it to the grandest stage of all thanks to you. It all came down to a T... Tatum! I love you baby.

I'VE KISSED ONE TOO MANY FROGS

By Aaron Woodson

(Frogs croaking)..."Ribbit, Ribbit!"

Sitting on the edge of a river, I look down into the tranquil waters and become reflective. The deeper I gaze, the more I come to realize that I'm soul-searching. Perhaps a miracle may travel down along a free-flowing current, just like when baby Moses journeyed the Nile in a papaya basket. Much to my chagrin, suddenly something leaps out @ me. For a moment, I'm temporarily startled. With somewhat of trepidation, I slowly become more intrigued with what I see. Instantly with a blink of an eye, I give chase to my observation. I make a move with a sense of urgency to try and capture what's been eluding me for so long. Just like that it slips away from my hands. When it comes back, I will surely be ready for its return next time... if there is next time. I've waited patiently all my life for this particular moment. It appears I'm playing make-believe, but it seems this surreal fairy-tale is one I've dreamed of in my sleep. Like a flashback, it all starts to come back as if it were a familiar episode that happened to me before. (Frogs croaking) "Ribbit...Ribbit!" What is that dreadful noise? It doesn't sound like crickets, but more like an orchestra of frogs trying to get my attention. For some reason these aren't your ordinary frogs, actually these frogs represent all the women I've ever kissed. They disgust me and it's no wonder I despise them. I've tasted their poison that comes from their lips which kept me under their deceptive spell. Their intentions were cruel and ugly...none of them really cared for me. These women are like a plague gone wrong. How long will it be before I'm rid of all these wretched frogs? All I know is I've kissed one too many frogs and it will be the very last time I ever will!

PRIORITIES

By Aaron Woodson

I know there was something I needed to do, but what? Oh wait, I have to do this one little thing first before I can do that...then afterwards I got to do something else! I almost forgot that I need to catch up on this other thing I didn't get a chance finish. Maybe next time. Okay, well let me check my schedule and I will get back to you on that! Doesn't that sound familiar to anyone? Hmm...sounds like there is a dilemma we all at some point in our lives experience...it's called priorities! We all get busy from time to time and it's completely normal. So where do we draw the line between procrastination and obligation? Perhaps we can meet along the inner lines of dedication and stop parallel parking next to our hesitations. With the help of a little meditation, we can achieve our certifications and gratifications. Time is our enemy and it doesn't wait for nobody. Take advantage of the opportunities that come your way. Remember that you are V.I.P. and that comes with some responsibilities. Handle what you can effectively control and let God take care of the rest. Understand and realize your limitations... you're only human, everyone makes mistakes. We often times can exceed our own expectations and make our ascension to higher dimensions. Never forsake yourself for another because you're simply too valuable to be placed below someone else. Most of us do what we have to do. Most of us do what we need to do. And yes, most of us even do what we want to do...almost any way! Priorities are appropriate and we have them for a reason. I make it a priority to be the man God has groomed me to be. And I make it a priority to put Him first! I'm not a part of a fraternity or sorority...I am my own entity! I am aware of my destiny...I know I am under the watchful eye of scrutiny...but as for my testimony, I will do what's absolutely necessary to make my life better. So, what is necessary? I'll tell you what it is... It's priorities that I speak of...that I live for...and that I die for!

SWEET REVENGE

By Aaron Woodson

You and I shared something special; perhaps we could have had a future together. But now that's all history. I live only in the present and your resentment for another led to us being separated. What I thought led us to having chemistry, only generated sweet revenge. You conspired to ruin our experiment and that cannot be tolerated. So frustrated that you would use me to get back at your ex. I realize where it all went wrong and now I'm left with it all just blown up in my face. Your motive was quite clear, but now for your final act...you must disappear. Easy come, easy go...you have no more tricks up your sleeve to use against me. Now how is that for sweet revenge?

COLD STARES

By Aaron Woodson

Is it just me or is it getting pretty chilly in here? Maybe it's whenever I walk by that some people give me cold, unwelcoming, piercing stares. I didn't know the temperature would drop so suddenly...maybe I'll crank up the Fahrenheit just a bit. If it's too hot in the kitchen, then you should probably get out if you can't take the heat! I know you are too busy sweating' me because you wish you were this hot. Don't be icy because you're not spicy. If you are reading this, then I'm more than likely talking to you and if you don't like it then that's too damn bad. Everywhere I go it seems like I get people staring at me as if they have a problem or they want to say something but just can't come out and say it. If you're going to stare at someone, at least make it known why you are staring in the first place. Seriously, you're obviously are staring for a reason...but please, don't be looking at me like a homosexual because I don't get down like that! Nothing against homosexuals, its just totally out of the question for me. I must be transparent to ya'll because you sure can see through me. Be careful when you see me next time because you might just end up turning to stone. Now how do you like that for a cold stare?

LOVE AND WAR

By Aaron Woodson

This is the story of a man marching to the glory of his destiny. As he engages his target, he is met with stiff opposition. The battle that takes place is between love and war. That is why we are all gathered here this very moment. We are fighting for the ones we love. There is no peace without the altar in which we may seek refuge from the evil one. My weapon of choice in this debacle is the power of the pen! For my pen is my sword and musket. I blast upon blasphemy, hate, jealousy, and treachery. Let it be known that I specialize in archery. Bring forth misery to the heartless all you brave hearts. This will be the day love conquers for all time. I won't take any prisoners, for love doesn't bind anyone in chains. I only want to capture my lady's heart...and that ladies and gentlemen would be my ultimate victory in love and war!

FALLEN OUT

By Aaron Woodson

Just when it seemed like I had fallen and couldn't get up...I realize that I simply grew apart from you. Now I can finally stand on my own because there isn't any more dead weight keeping me down. I sensed the pressure starting to build and something had to give. Our friendship, as a result collapsed like the World Trade Center. Once built on a strong foundation is now nothing more than a fragile sandcastle. Everything we shared is buried underneath...there is no chance of it resurfacing again. How did we end up this way? Like an elevator, what goes up...must come down. I never expected to hit rock bottom so fast. We will never reach the plateau where we were before. Permanent damage has been done and our fallen out will remain with us like the stain of tears.

FRIEND IN DISGUISE

By Aaron Woodson

It appears that we've agreed to terms of being friends. There is no shame in that except it only feels like a consolation prize. I'm a contender not a pretender. I thought we could come from the same blend and mix. You on the other hand, had other ideas. I'm only able to conceive the thought of us being more than friends. I was born to be with you. Don't you see? I'm more than what meets the eye...I'm just merely a friend in disguise.

CHERISH THE MOMENT

By Aaron Woodson

I'd rather cherish the love we've shared...then perish
from not knowing what could have transpired between
us. Where do we take place? The only locations that
it could happen would be our minds, hearts, and souls.
As we levitate to a higher inclination of love...let's not
transcend into the pitfalls of lust. Must we return to the
dust? We just only have begun to scratch the surface in
our quest for longevity. Trying to pick the right words
to say to the sky...I'm caught up in the wind like a kite.
You're the light I've been looking for and you guide me
through amazing heights. May we cherish the moment
we soared together into heaven until the end of time!

JOYRIDE OF FAITH

By Aaron Woodson

Cruising down a dark alley in a low rider, the wheels keep spinning just like my head often does. I drive down a path between tranquility and insanity, attempting to find a happy-medium. As I parallel park, I drop down the hydraulics of my thoughts and emotions. Stepping outside my exterior, I begin to examine my interior. In much need of a detail, I treat my joyride with the best of care. With thorough examination, there is something gets my attention. I notice the hub cap on the wheel is attached with numerous chrome spokes. Have you ever saw how every part of a vehicle functions with one another?

If something fails or goes wrong, other parts begin to wear out. Too often we rely on the high maintenance of mechanics...however, they can't fix everything. So how do we maintain ourselves and our vehicle? The answer is by having faith. Everything is connected to faith like chrome spokes attached to a hub cap. We can ride smooth, but sometimes it gets a little bumpy. We may get a flat tire at times, so we have to take it upon ourselves to change it out. Faith conquers doubt or speculation because it is self-sufficient and confident. This joyride of faith is like walks in the park...don't believe me, just try it for yourself!

EXCLUDE YOUR EX

By Aaron Woodson

Ever go to the store and purchase an item that had batteries included? Majority of the time they are both sold separately. Before we got into this relationship you invited me to be a part of your life. As time lapsed, our feelings for one another began to mix into this great chemistry. We found the right solution for experimentation...love! However, some things just simply don't mix, like your ex! He or she is past tense and I'm your present. There is no comma after me, just a period. We made our own sentence; he or she is just a fragmentation. Not trying to start a confrontation, but I need for you to deal with this distraction. Figure out this equation or there won't be a continuation of us if you're not willing to exclude your ex!

Elevator to Heaven

By Aaron Woodson

Going up or down? Let's go up. I've always wondered how many floors it took to get to heaven. Probably thousands of stories would be an accurate estimate. I look forward to meeting the great architect of this wonderful creation. The world appears immaculate with His touch of decoration. I will dearly miss gravity's pull as if it were a close friend called solid ground. However, I need to ascend to my destiny as I levitate through the clouds. I am moved through telekinesis and advance towards my new genesis! Reaching a higher altitude, I feel a powerful magnitude close by.... could it be what I think it is? Bright lights star power, everlasting melodies, angelic hosts, and last but certainly not least the Holy of all Holies! And to think all it took was one step in the elevator to heaven to get to this magical place.

FORTUNE COOKIE ☺

By Aaron Woodson

My dinner plate is stacked with such appetizing appeal.
My stomach has grown anxious from it's cry of hunger.
Without hesitation, I begin my meditation and satisfy
my appetite. I can taste the essence of China as I see
myself dwelling in their land. I sip the green tea that
flourishes within my soul! The seed is planted and I wait
patiently for my blessing. Little did I know, a brown-tan
like shell would change my life forever. With careful
examination, I cracked what was known to be called a
fortune cookie. As I read the message inside of it, I was
left with no choice but to embrace my newfound luck
charm. Misfortunes happen to people quite frequently,
but it will never stop the fortunes you're due to receive.
Believe and you shall achieve what you seek. Even if you
find it in a fortune cookie!

WISE BIRDS

By Aaron Woodson

It's been said birds of a feather flock together...but only the birds that are wise fly solo. The pressure the air brings, gives their wings the turbulence to rule the skies. At the height of their existence, they are the most regal of all creatures on earth. The wise owl perches high above the tree and keeps a watchful eye on its surroundings. The scent of foul decay brings forth the vultures as they lay claim to their feast. The hawk dives down like a 747 to catch their prey unaware. The crow scares off their enemies like it was a Halloween night. The penguin keeps cool and cruises like a submarine to catch its victims. The parrot keeps everyone amused by opening its beak and speaking for their audience. And who can forget the most powerful and majestic bird that exists? The phenomenal eagle; not only is it the wisest, but it's also the most fearless! My personality is like many of these birds and I inherit their abilities. Don't despise them because they are wise, open your eyes and listen to their cries. We should look to them as inspiration and not just for exploration. This is a dedication to all the wise birds that fly on their own accord!

THE FOUR F'S

By Aaron Woodson

I'd like to thank those that are here in attendance today...without you, writing this poem wouldn't be possible. Out of curiosity, what truly brings people together? There are holidays and special occasions that bring everyone closer. Perhaps an invitation from friends or loved ones may do the trick. However, there is something that attracts people to something I'd like to call the four F's. People just love the word "free" because it comes with no expense...not a dime... not a penny! They just show up and wait in line for free admission. They gather for food, free shows, gifts, money, economic security, and freedom. The gathering of food, whether it's weddings, barbeques, family reunions, holidays or baby showers; people always have to eat. Oh, let's get ready for our main event...a fight! We love to see some people go at it like a boxing match. Punches are thrown like flurries of lightening and feeling the pain of the fighter's leg is like a stallion's swift kick. Unsportsmanlike conduct is what spectators like to see. And last but certainly not least, we gather for the passing of one's life. We were featured in certain chapters of that person's life and now we have come to the end. As people gather today, we can send them on their way to heaven with prayers of love. How ironic it is that we are here remembering what brought us here...just think of the four F's...Free, Food, Fight, and Funeral!

THE DEVIL MAY CRY

Aaron Woodson

From the shadows to my dreams, evil lurks. Sinister
eyes observe my every move. An unwelcomed guest
trespasses against my will to serve Christ. For it is
he that opposes the righteous and the power of God.
Seeking whom he may devour, he roams the earth like
a lion waiting to pounce on an unsuspecting victim. He
may possess power on earth and command an army of
demons; but he is certainly no match for the all mighty
God and His heavenly angels. The sound of His holy
name makes the devil and his demons flee. He is a
coward and he doesn't fight fair. He retreats back to
hell and is constantly tortured for an eternity. When
the dust settles and the smoke clears, victory and
vengeance will be the Lord's! Trembling in agony, the
devil may cry in his defeat. The devil is burning all over
and He will reach a boiling point in Fahrenheit! May
the devil cry and burn to ashes!

REFERENCES

By Aaron Woodson

For many of us that would like to be considered, we have to state our credentials and references. Employers inquire about my character and skill from my references I listed on my application. If you really wanted to dig a little deeper, you should have asked me first. My character speaks for itself...no one can give you a better description of me rather than...ME! If you would have observed me during the interview instead of on paper, you probably would have hired me on the spot. Many people utilize references for certain reasons. Some have numerous references in their lifetime. Remember so and so...or what's her name...what's his name? Sound familiar to anyone? Some references are lost or forgotten, while others still remain on speed-dial or just a text away. We all have shared some of our personal identities with our references...they probably know just as much about you than you know about them. I'm sure you have heard this before, "I have a friend that I could introduce you to." "I think you should get with so and so." "He said...she said this!" Like a drop of a hat, we are so quick to blurt out a name. Here's a name you can give out...Aaron Woodson! I'm not just your reference, I'm your preference!

RELATIONSHIPS

By Aaron Woodson

Relationships are sturdy, yet fragile...they can be complicated at times where you don't know what went wrong. Where there are shattered pieces, there is glue to stick it back together. Most of us would rather retreat than make a stand for the ones we love. Relationships come with so many benefits, but also have their share of consequences. Security, self-worth, happiness, and love bring plenty of spring showers. Meanwhile, arguments and the lack of communication and trust lead to an avalanche. Some of us swing for the fence, while others strike out. In relationships, nothing is guaranteed... it's either a hit or miss! Like a curveball, you don't ever see the break-up coming. I might as well be placed on the Unable To Breathe List, because without you there is simply no air. Relationships have taught me to be stronger, wiser, and so much better than ever before! Relationships are like mechanics, they always need to be repaired. Without my toolbox, I can't fix the problems that require my full attention. Sometimes relationships have a flat tire...only you hope that you can find a spare. However, not all spares fit the way they should. The traction isn't the same and therefore there is no attraction. Relationships are like high mileage, sometimes they can run forever or they can simply run out their course. I'm not interested in any test drives; I only want to accelerate my relationship to the next level. Everything else bites the dust. Nothing else matters. It's all about me and you! If you want a lasting relationship with your partner, don't let these things destroy your relationship...Infidelity, Distrust, Jealousy, Miscommunication, and Grudges! If there is no trust, communication, respect, and love...you have nothing. Strong relationships are built on a solid foundation... not shaky ground. For the first time my feet are firmly planted on the ground and I know where I stand in my relationship. Do you know where you stand? Now is a good time to start!

ONLY WANNA BE LOVED BY YOU

By Aaron Woodson

As many people there are in this world, only one person has a place reserved in my heart. I welcomed her w/ open arms as she walked through that door and I've loved her ever since day one. In the twinkle of an eye, she made all my despair and loneliness disappear. I thought to myself, I must be dreaming…this can't be real. She appeared to me like an angel as if she were heaven sent…Where there was darkness, her beautiful smile overshadowed it. Where there was fear, she left no doubt that she be near and dear to my soul. Her love is one of a kind and not easy to find. She is exclusively mine and likewise I'm hers. She loves me the way that I am and has loved me like no other. There is no greater love and in my eyes she is extraordinary. How many of you only wanna be loved by that special person you're with? Take them by hand and show them how much you really do care and love them. Let them know how much they mean to you! Let them know that you only wanna be loved by them. Wherever you are, whatever you're doing baby, I'm reaching out to you. No one else matters but you because I love you Mrs Woodson! You complete me.

SOMETHING CALLED LOVE

By Aaron Woodson

I have been...I have seen...I have heard

about this thing called love. When I met her she was
full of substance. It wasn't by chance or circumstance
that I was caught in her trance. Yet it was the way she
danced that put me on to her beat. I took the necessary
steps to find out whether or not she was feeling me. The
clues she gave me told me everything I needed to know.
From that point, I amerced myself in what would be
the inevitable. With my adrenaline pumping, I reached
down deep for coverage and asked her to be mine. To
my surprise, she said yes. Within that moment I felt
like the sun had interrupted the moon and all the dark
clouds were lifted from my head. Nothing else mattered
because everything was aligned just like an eclipse.
When we first touched lips I began to see stars that
caused me to go into a morning daze. No longer did I
have to gaze at another sunset because now I have my
sunrise. Her light beams down on my mahogany skin
like brilliant radiance. I absorb her warmth like a

sponge. There was never a moment that we could ever dream of being apart. We became attached; we were one…which obviously meant we shared something authentic; something called love!

THE SORROW OF TOMORROW

By Aaron Woodson

Can I borrow a day of happiness? Everyday seems to
bring dreariness, so why must I be in fear of tomorrow?
Maybe because I refuse to go through another soap
opera in my life. Episode after episode brings yet
another program of drama. Must I tune in and see these
depressing events play over in my mind like flashbacks?
I clench my chest as if I were about to have a heart
attack. My life is in much need of restoration, the only
way to find it is through my exploration. I may not live
to see tomorrow, but tomorrow never dies as long as
sorrow exists.

THE LIVING ARRANGEMENT

By Aaron Woodson

Living in a house on the hill, trying to keep the peace
and be still. Starting to lose my mind with all these
distractions. Doing my best to hold it down for my
crew. Trouble is brewing and on the inside I'm stewing.
Bills come out of nowhere and have to get paid. Don't
ask for much except for a little respect when I come at
home. Too many disagreements over nothing, tell me
why can't we all just get along? I thought we were all on
solid ground, but come to find out we just didn't have
the right foundation. The walls are trembling and there
is a strong possibility of a collapse. Tried to make it
work, but everything about this living arrangement has
sunk down into the ocean.

NO WAY OUT

By Aaron Woodson

The system is designed for me and you alike to fail. Like a nail, they hammer us into the ground to hold us down. When can we set sail so that we can get out on bail to have a better tomorrow? I don't see that happening anytime soon. We are put in cages like savages and portrayed as animals put on display. So much ferocity and animosity among us, let's stop this and find a better way. Can't you see? They want us to put each other out of our own misery so they won't have to deal with us. For those people that are locked up for the crimes they committed, deserve to serve out their sentence. But sometimes we forget about repentance, the act of sheer forgiveness no matter what sin someone or even you may or may have committed. Who are we to judge? God says in Hebrews 10:30 (The Bible), *"For we know him who said, "It is mine to avenge; I will repay," and again, "The Lord will judge his people."* So who are we to judge anyone when we are all sinners? We have all fallen short of the glory and yet Jesus loves all of us beyond comprehension. In Romans 6:23, it says for the wages of sin is death, but the gift of God is eternal life through Jesus Christ our Lord. Sin separates us from

God, but God paid the price for our sins. He did this out of love so that we might be saved. In John 3:16-17, its states

"For God so loved the world, that he gave his only begotten Son, that whosoever believeth in him should not perish, but have everlasting life. For God sent not his Son into the world to condemn the world; but that the world through him might be saved." The only way to everlasting life is through Jesus Christ. He will decide our fate or you will choose your destiny, either way there is no way out!

A KNIGHT IN SHINING ARMOR

By Aaron Woodson

Once upon a time in the era of Medieval Times there were king's men dressed in shining armor that we know now as knights. They fought valiantly, relentlessly, proudly, and intensely for the sake of their country and for those they loved. When a battle was won, there was a great celebration. When they lost, all wasn't in vain because they lived to fight another day! Death was the only weapon that could stop a knight and there was no way a knight would back down from a challenge! Knights appeared menacing on the surface, but the way they fought was brilliant and often gruesome. Underneath all the armor dwelled a man that possessed a will to win and a burning desire within his heart. Knights always made a statement on the battlefield; they would kill to thrill the crowd. Knights were often feared, but received praise when they drew first blood. Victory simply wasn't enough for knights; they wanted to capture their ladies heart with their performance. And oh how they wooed them w/ their presence and charm; it's no wonder why they fell for them! These ladies received everything they deserved and could ever desire from their knight in shining armor. Emotions were worn on the knight's sleeve; his armor protected his heart and his helmet was his anointing. Knights stood tall and refused to take a fall except falling in love with his fair lady!

PROJECTED FORECAST

By Aaron Woodson

There is four seasons that we're fortunate to experience throughout the year. Unfortunately, we don't get the luxury to order the weather that we have...it's already been decided for us! Sometimes we can't get through the day without thinking about tomorrow. There are enough things that we deal concerning today and there is no guarantee that you will even live to see tomorrow! It's human nature for us to try and predict the who, what, where, when, why, and how. However, the variables more than likely will change.

Everything in life can be subject to change...we're not exempt. Like a projected forecast, fair-weathered conditions are not always present. There can usually be a reasonable chance of rain, snow, lightening, gusty winds, or hail. Everyone has their days...good and bad! Your altitude is determined by your attitude...you can expect to encounter some turbulence, yet it's how you maneuver through it that will keep you uplifted in this atmosphere. You may not be able to predict what happens to you, but you can change your outlook about the circumstance to go the distance. Don't base your life on a projected forecast because you may be disappointed with the end result. Rather, you should exhibit an attitude of humility and have the serenity to accept what is happening to you or what's happening around you!

UNDER PRESSURE

By Aaron Woodson

Before the snap, I can sense pressure coming from my
blind side...I know that in order for me to avoid being
tackled, I must make a quick and deliberate decision
to move away from the opposition. However, I
choose to stand tall and not fall...the ball is in my
court and I'm in transition to settle the score with
my life. I know I'm in the hot seat, yet I refuse to
get my ass cooked from all the criticism, favoritism,
and racism! I'm over the stove baking some hot
cakes while all ya'll over there cookin' up some
controversy! The media is like a drug dealer, they tell
you what you wanna hear and then supply you some
bullshit! Don't believe the hype, cuz once u get high
off those vapors, eventually you coming down from
that high! It's been said too much of anything is a
bad thing...I don't buy that because we all indulge
in some sort of recreational activity! Whether it be
money, sex, drugs, alcohol, politics, or whatever we
all use and abuse substances of any form! We all are
fighting through the storm searching for the calm
to our nerves! The alternative through the madness
is the faith to move the mountains in our lives.

At times life may send us an avalanche and we're buried under the pressure...however pressure builds diamonds and that exactly what we are...Diamonds that are under pressure!

THE GIFT OF APOLOGY

By Aaron Woodson

To the one I truly love and can't live without, please accept my gift of apology as a sincere token of my everlasting affection for you. I shed so many tears and put all my soul into this meaningful apology. Please open up the wrappings of my heart and witness the outpouring of unconditional love. I know I've paralyzed you from the neck down with my harsh words. I'm aware that I've used and abused you in so many ways. However, somewhere in this plague of darkness...the sun's rays shine through our hourglass. I got on my knees and sent up a prayer to our Lord and asked for His mercy. He was ever so gracious to forgive me of my sins. Now I'm asking for your forgiveness. In the event of my weakness, I need your sweetness to rain down upon me to wash away all this bitterness. I have had the pleasure to be introduced to your kindness, but without your love I'd go blind. I'm truly sorry darling and the only gift I could ask for is you!

EARGASM

Aaron Woodson

Psst...Lend me your ear; there is something you may
want to hear. Have no fear, because as long as I'm near
you will never have to shed a tear. I love you so much;
I'd share the last slice of my heart with you. Even if that
wasn't enough for you appetite, I would die and give
you every part of me. I know your ears are yearning for
a burning sensation. Love is in the air and your scent is
so pleasantly sweet. It only makes sense of why I'm so
attracted to you. Your love is intoxicating; it's no wonder
that I get a buzz. Like a radio station, I have a wide
range in variety. Tune in to hear my live broadcast of
sensual seduction. Fast, slow, high, low...that's the way
we like to go. Baby, echo out my name so that I know
that you came. Like a Q-tip, I keep waxin' until I give
you a good eargasm!

ISSUES

By Aaron Woodson

Can somebody please pass me a tissue for all these issues
we are having in the world today? Every time I look
around, there is always some sort of drama, controversy,
or conspiracy happenin' in this day in age. Like Marvin
Gaye said, what's going on? We live in a society of
flooded with issues like Hurricane Katrina. We are all
involved in this cesspool that's making us sink to the
bottom. Struggling to fight against the current, we need
to change course by going clockwise instead of counter-
clockwise! Time is not our ally in the circumstances of
our issues, yet we have to challenge ourselves to find a
solution to them. It's not always easy to find one, but
there is always one not too far away in our progressive
minds. Let us not be regressive in our thoughts and
lay them to waste in this pollution. Let us recycle our
trash and replenish ourselves from negativity. Our
subscription to everyone else's issues is not of our
concern; we need to deal with ours first and vice versa!
Just because we choose to label someone or something
doesn't mean that is what they are. If there are any

issues that I have, it's people that don't have a life and wanna live vicariously through someone else's life. So, my words to those people are to get a life and deal with your own issues!

CHANGE IS THE PERFECT STRANGER

By Aaron Woodson

Something has been on my mind for quite some time; I can sense that there is a strong presence on the horizon. Why am I threatened by the inevitable? Perhaps a thought conceived in my conscience tells me a change is soon to occur. My life and everything else around me will be affected by these drastic changes. Depending on your point of view, change can be good or bad. Nonetheless, we all must eventually accept change to be a part of our daily lives. It creeps on you like a stranger that you may not be very familiar with. Like a cold ice cube dropped in the back of your t-shirt, change can certainly send chills up your spine! Doesn't the thought of change give you goose bumps? Perhaps it may be the complete opposite as you may embrace it like a warm and caring hug. Change is very mysterious, yet we often remain curious or oblivious to what it brings…hope! Most of us may be on our last rope, but that doesn't mean you have to hang yourself from the gallows of pity and despair. Time to loosen the noose and swim down the river like a goose…just go with the flow!

There are times it will come very slow and at other times it will come very rapidly. You may feel that change is an inconvenience or that it disrupts your daily routine, but just remember that it comes like an unexpected visitor that only wants to greet you. Will you welcome change if it came knocking on your front door? If you can change your attitude everything else around you will begin to change too. Have you noticed that there is a Domino effect going on here? Don't be afraid of the transformation, we all go through the process…yet it all starts with you as being the individual. Look at yourself in the mirror and you will meet the perfect stranger from your reflection. Change is staring us in face; will we ever acknowledge its presence?

STAND YOUR GROUND

By Aaron Woodson

In this arena that we know as life, there are many
challenges that await us. Expect the unexpected;
be prepared to defend yourself when necessary.
Stand your ground! In every corner, nook, cranny,
and shadow trouble is always ready to get the jump
on us. Always be aware of your surroundings, this
world is filled with many traps that try to ensnare
unsuspecting prey. We may be the hunted, but the
hunter will soon become the hunted! Some of us
have a bounty for our heads, however a victory over
the oppressor is much more worthy and that much
sweeter. Don't give an inch of ground, this is your
land…this is the ground you walk on…this is the
ground where you stand! Mark your territory and
advance forward. Drive out those demons; block their
fiery darts with your shield of faith. Our Lord, our
God is with us in this very battle. Let your blade cut
them down to size. The word of God prevails in all
things, so use this to your advantage. "Man shall not
live on bread alone." As we thirst and hunger, not for
blood but rather for God's eternal word that we shall
be filled! The presence of God is upon us and now

our enemies have fled. We held up from the pressure and we were never moved. Men, we stood tall, we stood proud, and most of all we stood our ground! Amen.

CATS

By Aaron Woodson

Cats...every time I look around I see cats crossing in my path. Their hypnotic gaze stops me in my tracks as if to warn me to beware of these mysterious creatures. However, there is more to these felines than meets the eye. From what I've observed from their behavior, cats mostly like to keep to themselves. When I first tried to pet one, the cat turned down my act of affection by walking away from me. I learned very quickly that you're better off not showing cats any attention unless they want it. Women are a lot like cats, they can be feisty when they want to be. They most certainly know how to claw to the top to get what they want. They can often be shy at times, but at other times they know how to strut their stuff! And most of all they purr when you make them feel really good! There are all kinds of cats like cubs, kittens, tigers, lions, and cougars. I like the way a cat's hair stands so tall when they're frightened. My keen sense of awareness is aroused when her tail is up and twitching back and forth. When my pussycat walks near my path, something in my pants wants to stand up and dance. The dog in me has a bone that he wants to bury, so I ask her am I in too deep? She runs, but she can't hide...now I find myself chasing the cat!

Hate The Way I Lie

Aaron Woodson

When I get lost in your beautiful eyes, I feel like I'm
in hell because of the pain and torture I've caused you.
When you're hurting, I hurt just as worse. It's so sad
to treat the one you love like a dog that you kick when
you're in bad mood. How can you expect the person
you love to just roll over and pretend to play dead?
Treading mud all over the carpet is like wiping your
feet on someone's heart as if it were a doormat! It's a
low down dirty shame…How much lower will I go?
I've waited a long time for your entrance into my life;
however, from the way I've mistreated you I wouldn't
blame you if you were to look for the nearest exit! We
share the stage of love together and I can't see myself
moving on without you. We've been through the storms
and we've even been through the fire. We've come down
to the wire and my heart is beginning to short-circuit.
I'm desperate to repair two broken hearts along with my
own self-image. I hate the way that I am and I hate the
way I lie. I keep telling you that I'm going to change,
yet I keep doing the same stupid things. I'm willing to
change my ways for you and I apologize for every tear

that you've shed, for everything I ever said and done to ever hurt you.

I'm here now and I just want to make things right because I don't want to lose you forever. We've come too far to let everything slip away and I hope that it isn't too late. You're my soul-mate and I don't even want to think what it would be like to get to heaven's gate without you. It's been hell trying to get to heaven, but it's worth it as long as I have you in my life. I would rather die if you were not with me. That surely is no lie and I just hate the way that I've lied to the woman I love so much!

CAPTIVITY

By Aaron Woodson

As gravity pulls me down to reality, I realize that I'm under the thumb of subjectivity. Wrapped around the finger of constant accusation and affliction...I try to relieve myself from all this unbearing pressure. Painful words shake me like a powerful earthquake. Even a seismograph couldn't even measure my heartache. My walls begin to deteriorate with each passing day. There's got to be a way out of this captivity. I need reciprocity and deliverance from my depravity! I am looking for extracurricular activity from this mundane society. Please excuse my insensitivity to being placed under the microscope of scrutiny...I just have an allergic reaction to a world blind to captivity.

IF I WAS ON FIRE

By Aaron Woodson

If I was on fire, would you add more fuel?
If I was on fire, would you give me some oxygen?
If I was on fire, would you just stand there and let me
burn?
If I was on fire, would you pour water on me or just piss
on me?
If I was on fire, what would you do baby?
This is an emergency, can you please help me? You're
my 911 and we're on a hotline. The cause of this fire is
my yearning desire for your love. The longer I stay on
fire, the hotter and intense I'll become. Smoke begins
to fill the air and my eyes become watery. I'm getting
choked up and starting to suffocate. Let's touch lips and
begin CPR. You may find a pulse that will shoot right
through the roof! Truth be told, I can only survive in
the environment of your love. It's been said to be careful
when playing with fire because you may get burned.
Well, sweetheart my fire won't cause you any harm, it
will only keep you warm all day and night. I'm like a
blanket that protects you and wraps you tight. Baby, I'm
aware that I can be flammable but soon you'll catch on
to this flame. We're both one in the same...I'm your fire

and you're my desire! If I was on fire, could you stand the sight of me? I want to be the light of your world and keep your lighthouse shining bright forever! Please forgive me for asking you 21 questions, but I really needed some clarification. Let's be on the same page and not change the script. Let not our love be caged in lust, but return to the dust...in the form of ashes where they will scatter throughout the heavenly skies.

VOICE OF CONNECTION

By Aaron Woodson

Whose voice is being heard? Match the voice with
the name! Do you know who it is? I'll tell you…it's
the voice of me! Hear it..Feel it…and understand it!
I am one of many voices; however I am the voice of
connection! My voice speaks volumes and will endure
into longevity! God blessed me with a voice that will
echo throughout history like those that came before
me. I am the orator and narrarator, this is my story and
this is my life. You all should know that I put it down
in black and white…in living color…in expression…
and in truth! There are many ways of communication,
but I communicate most effectively in the lane of
poetry. Creative writing is my vehicle that takes me to
various locations. When you drive on the highway, pay
attention to the signs and you will see that my message
gets across very loud and clear! I challenge anyone;
know my voice because you will never forget the name
of Aaron T. Woodson!

LULLABY

By Aaron Woodson

As we lay on a soft, soothing, and comfortable bed...the feeling of tiredness falls on the two of us like the sound of a whisper. Each second that passes by we slowly fade to sleep. Before our very eyes close to sweet dreams, we sing a quiet little lullaby to one another. The sweet, but gentle words that we say to each other (*I LOVE YOU*) makes us drift into another place...heaven.

Deposit Slip

By Aaron Woodson

I just got paid and I'm ready to cash in. With check in
hand, I get in my car and cruise to the bank. As I step
on the scene, I make my entrance through the door,
passing by security. Before me is a long line of people
that are patiently waiting for service. So I stand at the
end of the line and then all of a sudden it hit me. Its not
what hit me, it's more like who did. I begin to assess
the situation that stands behind the counter across
from me. She is the best thing that I've laid eyes on all
day; I'm just standing there mesmerized by this pretty
young temptress. I'm only a few feet away from her,
but I sure would like to get in close by the inch. As
the line is moving along, I realize that I'm at the front
of the pack and next to be called. In my mind, I tell
myself repeatedly, "I hope she calls me over to her
counter." Much to my delight the most pure, magical,
and amazing voice called my name. Moving swiftly,
but with confidence I approach her with a broad smile.
She returns my gesture with a gleaming, yet friendly
smile back to me. She introduces herself and asks how
she can assist me. I tell her that I want to cash a check
and make a deposit into my account. So, she asks me

for my information and I have it ready to go. While she is helping me, I pause for a moment to check out her special features and focus back on her face. As I'm striking up a conversation, I put her on notice that she's caught my attention. By the time her eyes meet my gaze, it seems she almost knows that there is some sort of connection between us. This could really work out in my favor if I play my cards right. She completes my transaction and proceeds to ask me if there is anything else she can help me with. I grin and say, "Hmm...Well, you could help me by putting your number on this paper so I can maybe call you sometime." She pauses to think if she should really give me her number. With careful consideration, she smiles and decides to lend me her number along w/ a copy of my deposit slip. I tell her thank you, I'll call you! She winks at me and gives me a subtle hint of what I can expect from her smirk. I walk away triumphant from this wonderful encounter. If only she knew what I would like to deposit in her account. ;) She won't know what hit her and this eye candy will receive her deposit slip courtesy of her favorite customer!

PROCRASTINATION

By Aaron Woodson

Minutes are passing by like a high speed chase, hours fly by like the wink of an eye. Months of hibernation turn into years of fickleness and aging. Where has the time gone? Seems like the day was just telling me hello and then like a thief, night came and went without saying goodbye. How do we spend our time with each day? The days that we're given are very fleeting. They are like a first date that flirts with you and then leaves you no hope or guarantee of ever committing to you. The world doesn't revolve around us; we're on GT time... (God's Time). In the time that's made available to us it's to our advantage to make efficient use of it. We can't control the quantity of time; however we can demonstrate quality in our production. Results often occur when work is done. The process is of this action can suffer due to underwhelming achievement, lack of accountability, loss of desire, laziness, and the act of procrastination. It's a fair to assume, that we all have at some point in our lives procrastinated. During the course of each day and throughout each week, we know that we have certain tasks that need to be completed or deadlines that need to be met. Unfortunately, we sometimes fail to meet our expectations and delay or post pone everything else for a later date. However, the problem with that is when we put things off at the last minute we attempt to make up for lost time. Now here is where we get into a little bit of a dilemma, all that time we lost by not completing our objectives puts unnecessary pressure on ourselves which results in stress. This can simply be avoided with careful and manageable organization on our individual parts. Procrastination is a distraction; it's a setback that seriously jeopardizes our progression. Responsibility must be taken for our own actions and not blame anyone else or make excuses for our negligence. Procrastination is like a fault in the ground waiting for an earthquake to shake its foundation so it can finally be awoken. We need to stop slipping through the cracks and cement ourselves in success.

There is a difference between taking your time and procrastinating...which one do you do?

I'M DONE

By Aaron Woodson

I started out with one by my side, but now I stand alone. Been through the ups and downs, smiles and frowns. The circus came to town and finally it's hit the road. There are no more smoke and mirrors or stunts and acrobatics to perform. We juggled so much, but we couldn't keep up the act for long. Walked a fine line for quite some time, yet there was no way to balance everything between us. Even when we were hanging on by a thread, I tried to reach out but she slipped out of my grasp. Arguing became the norm for us and it was like an angry swarm of a wasp's nest. At some point, we were going to be stung by all of this. She was supposed to be my queen bee and all the honey we once had has now become bittersweet. The hive is no longer buzzin' and I've moved on. I won't ever come back nor have another encounter like this again. I had one, but she lost one. Neither of us won and separate ways we must go so that we can grow individually. Now I can officially say that it's all said and done. I'm done!

AWOL

By Aaron Woodson

You arrived in my life shortly after the departure of
your predecessor. You became the successor to my
fragile heart when you received the key. We were deep
in the trenches for quite some time now, trying to dig
ourselves out of this hole we created. At times we throw
dirt in one another's eye as we were quick to have one
another's back. Somehow fatigue must have set in as
you failed to report your absence. I was oblivious to
your frantic demonstrations of waving a white flag and
in the blink of an eye you deserted your comrade. No
letter, no phone call, not even an e-mail sent to my
inbox explaining why you abandoned me. You posted
your own bail and became a traitor to the love we
once shared. I feared this would have happened and
perception became reality. No reason to search for you
because you're not too far away. I can smell your guilt a
mile away. Did I mention you left your key? Next time
you shouldn't leave anything behind that you might
miss. Didn't even bother to kiss me goodbye, so now I
salute you from a distance.

WHAT COMES WITH THE PACKAGE

By Aaron Woodson

Ever go to the airport and go to baggage claim to receive your luggage? It's fair to assume most of you have. Most of us prefer to carry something lightweight, while others seem to carry more than they should. Life has a funny way of giving us an unexpected special delivery. I have been privileged to receive more than I bargained for. However, I'm happy with what I have and there are no complaints. If I want to keep what I have, I must be willing to accept the two for one package deal! There are no guarantees or returns…its either take it or leave it. Some people couldn't handle such a great burden so they bail out quickly. On the other hand, I stepped up to the plate and accepted this daunting task! There is a lot of work that needs to be put in, but overall there are very rewarding benefits. I have a package that is really unique and I already knew what it came with. It comes with more than anyone could ever handle…a ton of love!

Custody

By Aaron Woodson

As I contemplate my destiny, I prepare for the
inevitable…an imminent battle for the custody of my
child. Before you were born, I thought your mother
and I would help raise, love, and provide for you
together. However, your mother and I had irreconcilable
differences. We both tried to make it work, but we
continued to clash. It wasn't about you at all; you had
absolutely nothing to do with this. Just know that
even though your mother and father are not together
anymore doesn't mean that we love you any less.
You were God's gift to us and you still are…nothing
could ever replace you. As parents, we want what is
best for you. The fact of you not being in my life is
unconceivable. Obviously, the feeling is mutual where
your mother is concerned. Now you're all caught up in
the middle of this endless quarrel. We both want you in
our lives, but unfortunately you can only be with one
of us. I know it isn't fair, but here is a lesson for you…
remember that life isn't always fair. You're half of me
and the other half is your mother. The two of us became
one and eventually we split from each other which left
behind a seed. How can we blossom if we can't grow

together? Never in my wildest dreams was I prepared to be engaged in a custody battle with your mother. There is a possibility that I may lose this battle, but I will not quit and I will continue to fight for you. Whatever it takes, I will have custody of my child.

KEEPIN' IT CHURCH

By Aaron Woodson

I don't know what you all came to do, but for me praising God is mandatory! The glory belongs to Him and I will confess him with my mouth and believe Him in my heart. How many of you know Jesus? If you don't know Him, then I suggest you get to know Him. He is our Savior, the lamb that sacrificed to pay the ransom for our sins. Jesus loved us so much that He died for all of us so that we may not perish, but to have everlasting life. How good is He? It's so easy for us to look at the things we don't have, but sometimes we fail to recognize what we do have. We have a friend in Jesus that will never leave us nor forsake us. My brothers and sisters in Christ, we need to be in agreement with God and start loving one another. If you see your neighbor whose in need of something, why not lend them a hand and help them. There is a need for churches, for it is a place of fellowship, spiritual healing, and worship! I always thought of church as like a hospital; a place that gives holy treatment to cure the disease of sin! God founded the church and its purpose was to edify people. However, what I've noticed is that our government has attempted to silence the voice of the church. Its funny how today's society has been trying to phase out the church and separate it from state. Last time I checked we are all one nation under God! How can you take God away from something that He's already made and is in control of? You simply can't edge out God and for those that think they can are fighting a losing battle! Check your egos at the door and put Jesus first, followed by others and then finally yourself. The church is God's foundation and all his believers will continue to spread His message of good news to non-believers and other believers! For those people out there that think it's cool to burn down churches and vandalize them, don't think you have defeated us with your treachery. For vengeance is mine saith the Lord and His wrath will consume you like a blazing fire! Don't get mad at me, I'm just keepin' it church!

WHAT A MAN NEEDS

By Aaron Woodson

There comes a time in every man's life that his wants and needs should be fulfilled by the lady of his life. It's fair to say most men anticipate great things and want to be great in every way they can be possibly be. However, it's been said behind every great man is a great woman. Whatever a man wants or needs, a woman makes it greater and is the ultimate compliment to her man.

All men came into this world from the womb; they entered this life to be taken care of by a very special lady-his mother! Whenever he was hungry, she fed him. Whenever he was tired, she allowed him to rest in her bosom. Whenever he was sick, she did her best to take delicate care of him. Whenever he would cry, she made him feel better by saying or doing just the right things. Whenever he fell, she was right there to pick him up. And most of all, whenever she thought her baby was in danger she would be quick to protect him. The first woman that I loved was my mother because in my eyes she is the greatest. Most of her best traits come from my grandmother and I am truly blessed to have learned what love is because of my family. So, when the time comes, men will meet the love of their life and their counterparts should make every effort to give their men what they really want and need. Believe me ladies, if you do this majority of men out there will be grateful and return the favor back to you. If you're that special someone in a man's life, the first person he will want to introduce you to is his mother! Many women, especially men who read this will understand why mothers are so vital to a man's life. Unfortunately, some of us have lost our mothers or mother figures in life…but know this; they are now angels on assignments watching over you! Like men, women deserve and need love too. As men, let's treat the women we love not only the way we like to be treated, but also the way we would treat our dear mothers. The greatest need in this world is love; our chances of survival without it are slim to none. Love fills the void and it's a special gift that's been given to the whole entire world!

A Day Without Tay

By Aaron Woodson

Every moment I've had in this life, could never compare
to the day I met Tay. She is my Mona Lisa that makes
my heart smile. I traveled many miles to find her and
without a doubt, she was worth the wait. Heaven and
earth stood still from the moment we exchanged stares.
The starry glare from her eyes left me in a daze. A day
without Tay is like having no sun. A day without Tay is
like having no water. A day without Tay is like having
no air to breathe. A day without Tay is like having no
sugar to taste. A day without Tay is like having no rain.
A day without Tay is like having no good music to listen
to. Life has no meaning without her. A day without Tay
is like not having my morning coffee. A day without
Tay is like drowning in a pool. A day without Tay is
like not having my medication. She is my ceiling and
I'm her fan and I make sure to blow plenty of kisses her
way! I will love her til my hair turns gray. I look forward
to each day with Tay because a day without her just
couldn't be possible.

FRUITS OF PASSION

By Aaron Woodson

Of all the fruits I've ever tasted, you are the sweetest one
of all! Every time I think about getting a taste of you,
your flavor leaves a refreshing after taste in my mouth!
Like a ripe product that blooms in spring; you're the
special recipe that is full of the right ingredients. Each
fruit symbolizes its own significance to define passion.
Peaches are sweet, juicy, and round. Strawberries are
delicious, divine, and sexy! Cherries are always on top
and make everything just right. Kiwi is a fine blend of
relaxation and tropical storms. Apples get right down to
the core and never can be a sight for sore eyes. Bananas
are long, soft and creamy...they grow from all angles
as they dangle from every limb. When you combine
all these fruits together they make passion! Above all
honey, you are defined as passion. No fruit from any
garden in the world will do me any justice because you
are exclusively my fruit of passion!

MILLION DOLLAR DREAMS

By Aaron Woodson

To the bed is where I lay with the comfort of knowing that I will have extraordinary dreams tonight. I am nothing but just a simple man...an ordinary man. My aspirations are out of this world. I'm reaching for the planets, moons, and stars. There is no limit to where a million dollar dream can take you. What's even better is that it doesn't cost a thing. Investing in your future pays huge dividends in being successful. It all starts with planting seeds...keep adding to your product and you will reap what you sew. Dreams are the cornerstone for a lasting foundation. Nothing is easy as it seems... practice, repetition, and dedication gets you to where you need to be. Never let anything stand in your way. No one can tell you nothing. God is the true reason for your season. When praises go up, blessings come down from heaven. Seek first the kingdom of God and all these things shall be given to you. God gave men vision, if you can see it and believe it...you shall achieve it! Whenever you're out of pocket, just remember to hold on to your million dollar dreams.

DOOMED TO EVER FALL IN LOVE AGAIN

By Aaron Woodson

I've had many battles with love that would make most
people rattle w/ fear...So much wear and tear takes
its toll on one's soul. The pitfalls of love have left me
doomed to ever fall in love again. The one I loved
conspired to ruin everything we shared. Despite all
that has transpired, I happy to report that we are now
expired. What's next for a broken man? Whatever was
left of my heart is now in pieces. I believe love is an
endangered species...it's lost, long forgotten, and doesn't
live with me anymore. I can't go on pretending that
everything will be fine. I've locked the door and threw
away the key. No one will be able to bust in and get me
out because all my trust is gone. I am sentencing myself
to a lifetime of solitude. Forever I will be doomed to
ever fall in love again!

TRADING IN MY PLAYER CARD

By Aaron Woodson

Hey lover, I have something I wanna give to you. I'm
giving back my player card. I don't need it anymore
because I have something more valuable and authentic
that I could ever have...you! Since you came into my
life, I've become a changed man. I'm a better man
because you helped me find out what true love really is.
I'm very fortunate to have you in my life cuz without
you I'd be lost. I was in the game for fame...I was in it
for the highlight reels and stats. Had plenty of cheap
thrills that would give many people chills, but it's all
meaningless and trivial! I wouldn't deserve to be in any
hall of fame...I'd qualify for the hall of shame. Couldn't
blame you if you wanted to walk away from me now.

I'm officially retired from this young man's game...
you're wearing my number cuz you're my only one. No
longer am I playing the field...you're my shield and I'm
protected by your love. Please accept my player card as a
token of all my love for you. I'm trading it all just to be
with you for the rest of my days. I love you.

ONE CHANCE

By Aaron Woodson

If I had one chance, I'd ask you for this dance. By circumstance, you took one glance and I was caught in your trance. Let's go to France where you and I can simply romance. I'll take you around the world and into your final destination of sensation where we would call our dreams. Just one chance baby is all I need. Will you give me that chance?

RECOGNIZE THE FACE

By Aaron Woodson

In this crowded world we live in, one would think…
can't we all just get along? Unfortunately, that isn't the
case. Let's face it, racism still exists and it hits hard like
a fist. However, there are many twists to this tangled
web. Yet the issue of racism is quite sticky. Situations
can often be tricky when people get too picky with their
preferences. We are so quick to judge, but ironically
everyone will have to answer for themselves on the day
of judgment. There are many faces that come from
many races. We need to trace back to our history and
see that we are all from the same place. Many are lost
in the void of chaos and it seems their vision has been
distorted by these dark clouds. So tell me, do any of you
like what you see when you look in the mirror? We are
quite familiar with our appearance, but sometimes we
don't like ourselves for what we are. I believe if we took
the time to know ourselves, the better we would be at
getting to know others. Who are we to not like other
people? Despite our flaws and all, we are still human.
We're quickly becoming an endangered species by
voluntary or involuntary manslaughter…by abortion…
by domestic violence…by rape….by ignorance…by

destructive behavior…by evil…and most of all by lack of hope, faith, and love! We may be different on the surface, however we all bleed red. Water is blue and the stars and clouds are white…put it all together and we are one powerful nation! We don't have barcodes that we're scanned with; we're merely a social security number! We all are a member of society and yet there is so much variety. We all are marked like a bull's-eye and we have to watch our backs…but whoever or whatever may be targeting us make sure you recognize the face!

MILITARY APPRECIATION

By Aaron Woodson

Bow your heads and give a moment of silence to our fallen and beloved brethren. From the cradle to the grave, these men and women will always be known as heroes. Why is it that we can give them their flowers when they are gone, but not when they're alive to still be able to smell them? The feeling is bittersweet; lost in the battle, yet they have already won the war. Most people wouldn't or couldn't walk a day in these men and women's shoes...Dead or Alive! Every single day, military servicemen and women have fought for this country we call America. They have honored our nation and yet they don't receive the recognition that they truly deserve. When 9/11 took us by surprise, who was there to answer the call and defend our freedoms that we so richly desire and take for granted? You like to call politicians, musicians, athletes, and celebrities your heroes and worship the ground they walk on. Last time I checked we're the guinea pigs that are on the front lines! Where is our spotlight? I guess we're more visible during a time of war. Always under the microscope of scrutiny, yet somehow we've managed to adapt and overcome any situation or obstacle! We swore to an oath and no one put a gun to our heads to commit our lives to this profession…even if we die for it! That's how much we love God, you, our families, and this country. We support you…so why not support your military? A simple thank you would make our day! Ladies and gentlemen, thank you for coming out to show your military appreciation.

Anonymous lover

When I see you pass me by, I stop and think if I should
go out of my way.
So much I want to say, but I'm not sure how to
express myself to you. This is why I choose to remain
anonymous. You don't even know my name, so how
do I support my claim to not just be another guy? I've
seen men approach you and I can assure you I'm not
like the rest. I'm not saying I'm the best, I just have your
special interests at heart. For me, this is like taking a
test...whether I pass or fail, would I receive credit for
this course. Adding me and you together would bring
us closer to longevity. But so far, I've subtracted myself
from this equation. Perhaps with a little persuasion,
I can move the chains from a short-yardage situation
and get a first down. However, I constantly penalize
myself by holding back. I've been sacked and pressured,
all because of my own doing. Time is running out,
I must make a move. Out of desperation, I go inside
my playbook and dig deep by delivering to you this
anonymous letter. It reads:

"Dear anonymous,

I've wanted to reveal my true identity to you for quite
a while. I just couldn't find any other way but to do it
this way. I've seen you around and it truly brightens
up my day whenever I see you smile. I really like you,
but I just don't know how to bring myself to tell you in
person. Sooner or later you'll know who wrote this letter
to you. As well as one day we will meet face to face. But
for now, I must remain anonymous. We will always be
connected. Just in case you're wondering, we have met
before. Take care
(_____)

Signed,

Your Anonymous

TIME AND MONEY

By Aaron Woodson

Time and Money...essential to everyday life, yet
sometimes hard to manage both at the same time. Time
and Money have much in common but are also contrast
to each other. I was born within time and my tenure
here on earth is seasonal. Like time, I grew up around
money. Time and money were spent on me and I will
be spending much of that on someone or something else
sooner or later. Sometimes I wish I could trade time for
money or vice versa. Unfortunately you can't buy time,
so you must invest the time you have wisely. Money can't
buy you love because love doesn't cost a thing. Things
change, people change under the circumstances of time.
Money changes people and can be gained or lost in a
blink of an eye. Bills are mailed to us to ensure we pay
them on time. Money can be rewarded to us; however
time isn't so kind to return the favor. In other words,
time is money...if I had a penny for every minute I lived;
I'd be a rich man. Time and money can be your friend
or foe depending on your point of view. The way I look
at is time and money is an equal opportunity. Time and
Money is a formula for success. I play them both like
chess and keep everyone else in check!

Invisible Tears

By Aaron Woodson

Could you imagine yourself crying, but your tears just wouldn't take form? Let's take a minute to thaw ourselves out. Maybe we need to shed some light on this. Some of us have cried rivers…some streams…and even some oceans. There may have come a time where we had to sweat out our pain trying to cross the sands of time. Yet we are in a drought and the reason is we allow our feelings to dry up. I think it's fair to say most of us have cried two tears in a bucket and said "fuck it!" We hold back these tears so we show no weakness. However, the more we refrain, the more we are crying on the inside. Eventually, after all that pain is built up, it will erupt like a volcano and find its escape to the surface. We all are visible and vulnerable…we are human. How long can we cry these invisible tears?

STRICKEN

By Aaron Woodson

Dark Clouds clumped together, looking like the perfect recipe for a menacing storm. "There is a lightening watch, "the weatherman reports, "Be careful out there!" I'm not frightened in the slightest; in fact I will wait for its arrival. In my hands I hold a bottle and I will trap a bolt of lightning in it. Attempting to avoid being struck, I dodge it like I was escaping a bullet. I'm wondering if lightning strikes twice in the same spot; immediately without hesitation I retreat back to my original location. Suddenly as if the lightning responded to my challenge, it rapidly flashes down to strike me in my own heart! The electricity begins to flow through my veins and its driving me insane. The power is immense and I can't withstand its mighty force. I'm stricken and as the plot thickens, I think to myself whatever hit me must have been God!

HONEYMOON ON THE MOON

By Aaron Woodson

You and I have taken that long walk down the aisle.
We've been together for awhile now and shared
pleasant memories. So, what's next for the two of
us? Maybe we should start with our honeymoon.
Make no mistake though, this isn't any ordinary
honeymoon. This one will surely be one to remember
for the ages. This will be written in the pages of all
the history books. Without any further delay, it's
time for me to fly you to the moon and then we
can go visit the stars! I expect an estimated arrival
time of about noon. Shortly after we'll cruise in the
limousine and feast on a fine cuisine. From there
we can pop champagne and toast to the good life.
In our celebration, I've decided to croon a soulful,
yet beautiful song just for you. It's called "Honey I
Do." The moon is my center stage as I glow in it's
spotlight. Flowers, cards, and candy is simply not
enough, I really need to show you how I feel about
you. Crawling inch by inch to you, I begin to cry
white tears that stain my cheeks. Pouring from my
face to the ground, it seems as if I'm drowning in a
sea of milk. Then I begin swimming over to you like

sperm racing to an egg. When I finally reach you, our lips touch and honey starts to spill out from our mouths. Never could we imagine honey being on the moon...hmm, how sweet is that?

DAMAGED BEYOND REPAIR

By Aaron Woodson

When we became deeply involved I already knew I was at a disadvantage. The relationship we had was like a used car, we knew we'd encounter some problems eventually. On this journey called love we blew a few tires on so many rocky roads. We left leaky trails with each path we crossed. Tried so many times to jump start this dead battery but to no avail…our transmission finally decided to give out. It's damaged beyond repair and we are no longer serviceable to one another. Sometimes the lights aren't always on upstairs, and like a deer in the headlights we got ourselves into a wreck! This was accident waiting to happen and now I'm crushed. There is no way we can even begin to salvage any part of this relationship now. Everything is up in flames and smoke…even the firefighters would have a hard time putting out this fire. Love isn't bulletproof, fireproof, or even waterproof for that matter. It takes its lumps and bruises as you're trying to hold on for dear life. Sometimes it felt as though we were on life support. Most of the time that is the only thing keeping you going momentarily, but we've already killed ourselves trying!

MEMOIR OF A VET

By Aaron Woodson

I moved out of the state with a new state of mind.
Left all the baggage behind, the South had welcomed
me with open arms. The city of Jacksonville's charm
has left quite an impression on me. St. John's River
flows through the heart of the city. The humidity
greets me no matter where I go. The Landing is such
a hot commodity, the scenery is breath-taking and I
enjoy being a part of this wonderful community. The
one thing I haven't been immune to has been natural
disasters such as hurricanes. The rains come and the
winds blow...we are in the season of the end times.
Storms arrive with very little notice, but they always
seem to send a very powerful message. I always try to
remind myself that these storms won't last...they too
shall pass! I haven't seen any mountains here, but I
sure have had some to climb in my life. I've been at the
bottom and I'm making my way up to the top. I don't
want to be on a slippery slope and I've never been a
dope boy. I just want to be like a dough boy and make
more bread that I can count. I've always wanted to
amount to something...my value is priceless just like a
diamond. I've had to get cut and handle the pressure.

I've got great ambition for good measure, still looking for my treasure. I think about it night and day like Al B. Sure…just thinking of when she will come around. Guess I have to wait my turn with this crazy Merry Go Round! God knows my heart, I've been down on my knees praying He makes my dreams comes true! Cried many of times, some tears were from me singing the blues and paying my dues. Other times they have been tears of joy…I realized you can't let anything or anyone steal your joy! Life is all about investments so make a deposit of love and keep a savings account filled with it. Remember my friends love always pays off, but it takes work. Change your mindset and focus on the good. Be thankful for your blessings and take nothing for granted. It's a new day…write a new beginning. Don't wait, start now!

TO PROFIT OR BE A PROPHET

By Aaron Woodson

I always dreamed to make a profit and fatten my
pockets to be on sumo! The words I speak into existence
known as affirmations are revealed by a modern
day prophet. There is power in my words to move
mountains, yet I still have to climb Mount Everest.
The most difficult challenge of achieving greatness is to
keep going through your journey to reach your desired
destination. I've always been fascinated by these dollar
signs ….wealth is good for my health. My plan of attack
is to be in stealth mode. They say the ones who flash
surely never last. In life you can be certain about the
dash between your birth and death date. Don't forget to
bring me flowers while I can still smell them before it's
too late. Just like a butterfly we all go through stages.
As Shakespeare once said, All the world is a stage and
everyone has their part. I always wondered would it be
better to die being broke or die with a broken heart?
Now which profits or prophets do I choose?

ALL HEARTS MATTER

By Aaron Woodson

Let's get something clear right now...ALL HEARTS MATTER. All this chatter about hearts being broken and hearts on the mend is crazy. Real love is never lazy; true love is always at work! If two people love one another then both hearts are responsible for each other. Hearts are strong and they always know who they belong to. Two hearts beat stronger than one. Every heart has a love song...its meant to be sung to the one it sings about! No matter the distance or geography, love knows no boundaries or limits. Like Wi-fi, hearts that love each other connect on the same frequency. Hearts communicate and are fluent in the language of love. Hearts have no bias. Hearts mean more on Face book than likes. ALL HEARTS MATTER and deserve respect. The world suffers from heart attacks and heart disease...but I tell you we need a heart transplant of love...a heart transfusion of compassion and a shock of God's touch to revive us! The heart has four chambers and it circulates blood flow and oxygen to vital organs in the body. Hearts are not just anatomy...its monogamy and harmony twisted together like strands of DNA as one! ALL HEARTS require intimacy...they are relational and everything hearts do is intentional. Love is unconditional and unconventional. Nothing about falling in love is controversial or partial. HEARTS ARE MADE TO BE WHOLE. Just like all lives matter…ALL HEARTS MATTERS! Let's not forgot ever forget that!

THE INTERVIEW

By Aaron Woodson

Everyone has a story that they tell so well. If anyone
were to ever interview me, I wonder what I would be
asked. I'm sure I would be expected to give detailed
answers to some probing questions. I've found that most
people in this world are very curios. We often just can't
help ourselves about discovering things about people
that pique our interests. Stories are intriguing and
gives people insight on what is occurring at the time
or shows the character development of the person. The
most important thing about a story or interview is to be
authentic and just be unapologetically honest. However,
you must always be careful what you reveal because
it can be a double-edged sword. Don't incriminate
yourself, yet be genuine. So why don't we get started
with the interview...ask me anything you want!

STAND AND DELIVER

By Aaron Woodson

Stand up or take your seat…if you really wanna make
a difference put your money where your mouth is! Now
is not the time to be on the sidelines, real leaders lead
from the front. Don't retreat in defeat unless you're
certain of victory! History always seems to repeat itself;
the past has paved the way for the future generation.
We are suppose to be a democracy, where everyone has
a voice…but we all know who calls all the shots. I am a
citizen of this country known as the good US of A…I
have fought and served and served for this country
that I love. I was part of the 1% who took the oath and
stood alongside great men and women who shared the
belief of truly making an impact. We are her defense
and I take great offense to politicians saying we need to
make America Great Again! I also take offense to those
who always have an opinion or something to complain
about but never have any solutions or contributions
to the cause. Oh the hypocrisy! America isn't perfect
by any means, but she is certainly beautiful and we're
sewn into her vibrant fabric known as freedom. What
started out as segregation has now become integration.
All this talk about immigration…well let's just set the

record straight, we are all immigrants...this country was founded on it. We are all pilgrims basically strangers passing through this earth. Let's not allow ignorance to keep us divided and let's not have a biased society! Various issues strike our curiosity. While the majority of them are important and should be addressed, remember not to lose focus on the bigger picture. Our lost and dying world needs a healthy generosity of love, kindness, peace, and happiness. May we be advocates and ambassadors for reciprocity, diplomacy, and hope for the atrocities happening in our world. We can no longer sit idly by...it's time to take action and bring forth justice and change. We are not the silent majority...I'm a minority and I'm taking a stand. I have spoken into existence that I will change the world. I WILL STAND AND DELIVER!

For You, Prince

By Aaron Woodson

April 21st 2016…is a day that shocked the world, such a
sad and tragic occurrence. The Artist Formerly known
as Prince passed away. The world was truly bathed
in Purple Rain; It almost seemed as if time paused
for a moment to grieve and remember the legendary
musician. Prince was massively influential in pop
culture and he changed the whole musical landscape.
He was transcendent, magnificent, dynamic, bold,
brilliant, innovative and a musical genius! At the
same time he was like a magician who dazzled you on
stage with his creative wizardry. His Royal Purpleness
was born a star from his hometown of Minneapolis,
Minnesota. Prince left an invaluable and enduring
impression on us. His spirit will live on through
his numerous collections of songs that he recorded
throughout his lifetime. Such a dimunitive figure,
yet his presence was larger than life. Like his song, I
WOULD DIE FOR YOU, he did exactly what the
title of the song implicated. Your fans are still calling
your name and they still want to go crazy! The elevator
could never bring you down, but the irony is that your
body was found near the elevator in you Paisley Park

estate. Perhaps, you were taking the elevator straight up to heaven. The day you died seemed like a song you wrote called SOMETIMES IT SNOWS IN APRIL. Somehow during that tragic day, a beautiful rainbow appeared over your estate. It was a reminder that it was a sign of the times. Your music will always reign in my heart and just to let you know...your fans really ADORE you! Rest in paradise our dear Prince!

WRECKLESS TESTIMONY

(Freestyle) "True Story"

By Aaron Woodson

Got me gassed up, foot on the gas petal
I'm still coming with that velocity
Coming with that ferocity
Ain't with that mediocrity
Can't be associated with that atrocity
I'm from the city known as V-town 707
Shout out to the Bay
All these years I stayed in my lane, but one night it
almost ended on Interstate 80. Got caught swervin,
flipped over in the Benz 3 times! Saw them Sparks
like Jordin...life flashed before my very eyes! Lucky
for me that seatbelt came in handy. Laid out in the
Johnny Blaze fit, could've went out in ablaze from
that wreck! Blood on my Lugz sneakers...it was a cold
night when God came to me and my friends rescue.
EMT's rushed me to the emergency room, couldn't
talk...mouth full of dirt. Family came to visit me in
the hospital, their reaction was priceless...released
that same night!

Thank God...so blessed to be alive today, always knew I was a survivor! But at the end of the day, I was so wreckless! Crashed but didn't burn. The story didn't end, it had to continue!

Brutally Honest

By Aaron Woodson

If I'm brutally honest, I'd tell you to go to hell....but
surprisingly all I can do is wish you well. People come,
people go. Some stay for a season, some stay for the
trilogy. That's the way it goes...the world can be bright
one moment and turn dark the next. Now excuse me
while I flip on the switch, I need to expose some things
to the light. By no means am I perfect man...I make
tons of mistakes, I've hurt, and disappointed many
people. But all of that doesn't define my true character.
People often sleep on the good you do and your good
qualities about you.They are blind to their own flaws,
yet wanna call you out on yours. The tongue carries
venom, it's like life and death. I want to speak life but
right now I'm not in my right mind or in the best of
places. I see fake faces all around me. So now I'm trying
to find one face that will be true to me. I'm tired of the
flakes, fake handshakes, fake hugs, and empty promises!
Real eyes that cry real tears recognize real lies! You can't
fool me, I see through the facade. Stop pretending to
put on an act...put some respect on my name! You think
you hurting me, but really all your doing is hurting
yourself. Some wounds are self-inflicted, but others are

inflicted from people like you! It will take time to heal all of this, it's a process. I am very resilent...every minor setback is a setup for a major comeback! This is my clap back....I could ruin you, but God has shown me grace and humbled me. I extend grace to you because of what my Father has done for me. Be thankful I don't seek revenge. The battle is not mine it's the Lord's. I know God will deal with you and maybe you'll change your ways. So with that said, I've said my peace and I was brutally honest. I'm praying for you...but to my prayer warriors out there keep praying for me and people that need it. Amen!

HENNESSY

By Aaron Woodson

Excuse me, can you tell me where I may find some Hennessy? I seem to have this spell binding attraction for her. She comes only in a few ounces, but she can certainly pack a punch! Her name echoes like pure bliss and I get weak in the knees for her. Hennessy is my preferred choice because she is so regal and divine. She leaves me with an unforgettable impression. It's definitely been a pleasure and privilege to have known her so intimately. Each sip takes me on a trip that's out of this world. I float on air every time we are together. We celebrate through the good and bad times and she brings me joy and comfort. I never have to look too far for a companion because she's always been there for me! She is more than a fine cognac, she is my sweet Hennessy and I truly adore her.

ALL VOTES MATTER

By Aaron Woodson

People are scraping just to get by. Hard work is where the rubber meets the road. I'm driving down the interstate and I exit off on Opportunity Boulevard. I notice that some of us are jammed up in traffic, trying to navigate and find our way. Seen too many stop signs, we need to find more green lights. Hope is in sight and the sun is shining upon us. A signal of a new day, we can make it through any kind of weather. Nothing can ruffle these feathers. Our people are tougher than shoe leather. Fists raised in the air like Muhammad Ali…we were born to be champions! Oppression will be defeated and Freedom will be our victory! The struggle has been real, but it hasn't stolen our joy! We are in formation and have employed our strategy. There has been some noise in these streets, yet we remain poised and determined. We won't undermine authority, but we ask you just listen and hear us out. We are not asking for a handout, we are asking for a hand up! If you want us to cooperate with you then we ask you to cooperate with us. No need to complicate matters with unnecessary acts of violence, fears of retaliation, threats, etc. Let's be humane, don't be insane…it's time we use our brain.

Vote for the right candidate to lead this country going forward and beyond. Let's not continue to get sucked into the vacuum of lies these politicians deliver to us. Go to the polls and use good judgment. It's not about popularity, this is about the majority. Some of us are minorities but we still play a vital role in the bigger picture of things. ALL VOTES MATTER!

The One That Got Away

By Aaron Woodson

I remember like it was yesterday, we went to the same school when we were young kids. I always had the pleasure of seeing you in class every day. You were about 5ft nothing with long pretty dark brown hair. Slender from top to bottom, yet even then you a lil' somethin' somethin. You were definitely a sassy one but a classy one. You reminded me of the late singer Aaliyah. You were One in A Million except you were Caucasian mixed with some Latina. It's funny how you and I were voted teacher's pets among our classmates. After elementary we went our separate ways only to reconnect in our later years. To this day we still talk here and there. Somehow you always knew I had a crush on you. I'm so proud of you. You have two beautiful kids of your own. I see they growing up and they look more and more like you with each passing day. Sometimes I wonder what the future would have been like with us being collaboration. We would have been a terrific pair. Nothing else compare 2 you. I often reminisce and I come to this conclusion every single time…you're the one that got away!

FIRE & ICE

By Aaron Woodson & Sylent Lampkin

I clean up nice…suit and tie…you might say my game
is Taylor Swift…Swift with the pen…slow to offend
but make sure I put my hands together at night…and
never forget to say Amen…Like J. Cole I got dreams
to catch…sailing on my own wave of momentum. I do
this night and day…then say or speak it Al B. Sure…
My words will go platinum as I penetrate precept and
concepts of these ladies craniums…I'll throw some
D's on it and make em' disastrous in denial while
being dangerously delirious…Oh baby, you know I
can be serious…leaving you all curious and turn out a
performance like Fast and Furious…Like Tech Nine,
I gotta beat it up and make the hood go crazy…Tryna
catch me ridin' dirty…got the sound of revenge blastin'
inside your walls like an 808. Ahh…wait a minute don't
say shh…hear me coming like I got that thunder…I
bring that fire, my ace is known as ice…Two giants in
the game coming together to makin' the perfect storm!
We're in our element, rockin' a pair of Jesus pieces…
better bow down to the Underground Kings of Poetry.
We so trill and still going hard in the paint. Going
ballistic on the mic, sending torpedoes and scud missile

lyrics on you suckas! When we show up, we blow up.... its pandemonium! Like Tuskegee Airmen, we stay droppin' bombs on our foes. We're the heroes and you're the hoes, now see whose exposed? You don't want it with Fire and Ice! *DROPS THE MIC*

WERE YOU THAT GUY

By Aaron Woodson

Being a great guy doesn't mean you'll always end up
with the girl. Being a great guy just means you're a great
guy...nothing more, nothing less. She doesn't owe you
anything or need to do you any favors. On to the next
one, gotta check for new flavors. I'm an acquired taste
to most women I meet...some love my style, some knock
it. I'm eclectic and versatile...got my swag on, rockin'
the snap-back w/ my arm out the window. Cruisin
down the street in my G6, yeah I manuever slow. So
let's start the show...I got the flow to make the right one
weak in the knees. She stay in that position when she
pray to the man upstairs! Oh yes she's blessed to be in
the presence of a king....God knows we're a match made
in heaven! For years I came off the bench, but now
I'm a starter and I'm just getting warmed up! No more
rejections at the rim...I shot my shot, damn can't believe
it went in like that. Now I'm still in my lane driving
down the floor, leaving all these broads shook...took it
straight to the hole and hit a slam dunk! I'm the daddy
on this court...no more playing games! Hittin' all these
thots with a Tech! I'm a player and a referee at the same
time...I always call it down the middle. Yet sometimes it

don't always go your way...so you gotta man up and try not to cry foul! Sometimes you will take an "L". Other times you will be winning and grinning...celebrating with your arms embracing your trophy. But in the end of a long season, was it really worth it? Were you that Guy?

THE ENCOUNTER

By Aaron Woodson

I knew when I first saw you, I had to know your name.
This isn't a game, I'm for real. I would never waste my
time or yours...I am very interested in you. How can I
make you see? You can see the lames a mile away...but
not every man is the same. I want to stand out to you
and reveal my true character! Most men are advertised
in a negative way...I want you to explore me as much
as I want to discover you. Your eyes fascinate me...
they draw me in close like a moth to a flame. Your
smile captivates me and shines bright like stars above.
I love constellations in astronomy...I feel like I'm in
your orbit looking for a place to land. So I guess I'm
too busy concentrating on you for the time being. In
space there is nothing but time, but here on this planet
time keeps slippin away. I want every second to count
when I'm in your presence. I have no agendas... just a
man who has a plan that wants to include you into his
life! I know you have your boundaries and guards up, I
respect them. Please let me show you that I can handle
any obstacle you put in front of me...I bet I'll find a way
to your heart! There is nothing wrong with me being
attracted to you or you being attracted to me...this

only comes naturally. God didn't put us in each other's path by accident. I believe your spiritually made and tailored for me. But I'm gonna pray on it and let God decide and you should too! I'm not a perfect man by any means...have compassion on me as I will do the same for you! I'm working on being a better me...maybe you're working on a better you! Together we can grow much stronger...we can take our time and invest in each other! In the Word, it says store up your treasure in heaven and there your heart will be also. You're my treasure I'm storing up because I know I'll see you again in heaven. I Thank God we met and that you came into my life. I believe someday you will be my wife...but until that happens I'll be waiting for confirmation from God!

CONSEQUENCE OF LOVE

By Aaron Woodson

Life has its rewards, but there's always consequences
that go with it. At times things in your life can be
balanced which is known as order. And other times
things in your life can be imbalanced which is known
as disruption or chaos! When I first spoke your name
there was meaning. I called you into the light because
you were a beautiful sight to behold. Have I told you I
love you? I chose to fall for you...and fall I did. It was
all roses in the beginning, but I realized too late that
you came with thorns. I got wounded from your sharp
touch. Love made me blind like Stevie Wonder...I made
a choice and it turns out you were the wrong one. You
live and learn...that's my consequence of love I suppose.

IF I'M HONEST

By Aaron Woodson

If I'm honest, all I see is changes. Nothing remains
the same except for the one up above! He know about
my sorrows, but I know tomorrow will be a better day
if I'm blessed to even see it. Yesterday is long gone,
its in my rearview. Today is here and seems clear that
I have a long way to go in this life. God only knows
what my future will look like, its in His hands...I have
no control over it, I've learned to submit. I have to
decrease so that He may increase. Not my will, but His
will. This walk hasn't been easy...been a few bumps in
the road. Some pain and definately lots of struggles.
I've even fallen down a few times and sometimes
lost my way. Its always been just me and God. I've
always looked for support, but I had to learn to rely
on Him and no one else. Many times I felt anger or
discontentment because I felt forgotten or disregarded.
Yet God never took His eyes off me...He never left me
or forsaken me. He is with me. But now I'm doing
just fine. I realized God doesn't need any help to deal
with me. He's got this...and I know with His help I got
this too! Some have wished for my downfall, but this
is only the beginning...what they may have meant for

my harm, God intended it for my good! His strength is more than sufficient in my weakness. I can do all things through Christ whom strengthens me! He saw the best in me and He is the best for me! Amen.

DISTANCE WILL NEVER BE RESISTANCE

By Aaron Wooodson

I've known some people for a number of years...yet I don't recall ever seeing their phone number pop up on my caller ID. We all went our separate ways and got disconnected. Tried writing you letters but got no reply. Alas, all I can do is sigh. Life goes on...the wind blows behind me. I'm soaring to new heights and been gone like the wind. I often wonder how you're doing over there. I pray that we will be reunited again. I hope that will be the outcome. Or perhaps not...regardless you still are in my heart. Dearly departed, don't forget about our wonderful story we shared together. We made it through the past...but forever we'll always last! Distance will never be a resistance.

THE TRUTH ABOUT LOVE

By Aaron Woodson

I used to think love didn't come at a price...but how naive I surely was to think like that. I've realized that love in fact does come at a price. There is an investment you have to be willing to make when it comes to love. There is even a better word for it and that's called sacrifice. People say you can't help who you fall in love with. I have to disagree...you can help who you fall in love with.

You are free to choose who you love. Love comes with great responsibility. You have the ability to love with all your senses, yet you can also be under the spell of love's influential power! Love is like a double 2-edged sword... it cuts deep and penetrates the inner most soul! Truth be told, love can almost take you hostage or it can release certain inhibitions. Nowadays people hesitate or question if love is worth the risk. Painful hurts can often leave us in a crippled state of despair. Hearts often need repair...broken hearts heal stronger in time. But in the meantime, we gotta keep our guards up.

Love is a battle sometimes. It isn't always pretty...the ugly truth can be exposed. However love can bring out the best in us...we stand and take everything love gives us. I've learned love endures and if you can withstand the pressure, we can make it through anything. Love can change hearts...it can bring happiness, peace, hope, and faith to our lives. At times love is gentle but the fight for it is certainly intense and epic. You give everything including your last breath for love!

Jesus best demonstrated this as he died on the cross at Calvary. He died because He loved all of us so much. He also forgave us of all our sins. No greater love is there than one who lays down his life for his friends and family. Love is a gift and its meant to be shared with the whole world. Love is our compass...let it guide you and let it consume you. Love will help you find your way. Love is here to stay. When it's all said and done...love will always be the answer! This is the truth about love.

LABELS

By Aaron Woodson

Labels...When I think of labels, they are most often
associated with a particular brand. Labels can also be
a stigma that is given to a particular person or group
of people. Most people shop for the hottest and newest
labels like Michael Kohrs, Air Jordan, or Apple. Those
kinds of labels have a great reputation because it's a
trusted commodity among consumers. People buy
into labels...sometimes those same labels are falsely
advertised among the general population. Labels are
in competition with each other and try to woo people
onto their collective side. Some people have labels
unfairly placed upon them because others choose not to
understand where those people are coming from. Labels
are titles that are man-made. Labels are temporary, they
aren't guaranteed. Most people place so much value on
labels and not enough on other people. This is what
is known as materialism and superficiality. At birth
we were given a name, that's it...nothing else needs to
be added unto it! You didn't need a label before and
you don't need one now! Labels can be uplifting or
condescending...they can give praise or make you feel
shame. Labels can also give you fame...but your name

is more than enough recognition in anyone's lifetime.
Your name comes with value...know your worth!
Remember the name of Jesus is above all names...
he didn't need or have any use for labels or titles. He
referred to Himself as I AM! Drop the label and ask
yourself this question...What do you refer to yourself
as? Let that be your introduction and let it carry you
until your conclusion.

TAKE OFF YOUR MASK

By Aaron Woodson

She disguises how she truly feels about me by being passive-aggressive. I see through the act, you know you want me. Stop pretending you don't care about me... you're just lying to yourself. I won't force the issue. I just know all the hurts your carry may call for a tissue. I'm here for you...but I refuse to be the scapegoat for what someone else has done to you. If you're serious and want this to work, then you'll know where to find me. I won't be far...but I hope you'll consider drawing near to a love you've never quite known. Now is the time to take off your mask!

My Proposal

By Aaron Woodson

I wore a tailored suit and tie, already groomed for my future bride. I swallowed my pride and got down on one knee. It almost feels like I'm auditioning to be her leading man...I have to make sure I give her the best proposal of a lifetime. She looks me dead in the eye...I look back at my destiny, tears in the wells on my eyes. The moment is so emotional for me, I take my time as I speak these words to my future wife. "You're my best friend...you're my inspiration...you're everything I could ever want, need, dream, and hope for in a woman. You make me feel alive when I'm with you. You bring out the best in me, you understand me most times when I don't even understand myself. You're the missing piece to my heart's puzzle. You're the key that unlocks all my mysteries. You're my moon, my sun, and the stars... none shine brighter than you. Love has been calling my name for awhile now. I can't ignore that its been knocking on my door. Well, baby that was you...I had to welcome you into my life and as they say the rest is history. I couldn't think of anyone better to spend the rest of my life with and be committed to forever! I love you! Will you (bride's name) marry me?

You're on Camera

By Aaron Woodson

Your always on camera. All eyes will always be on you! Privacy is becoming a lost art nowadays. Selfies, profile pics, interview pics, text messages, surveillance videos are all caught on camera. The camera doesn't lie. Cameras expose you...never forget that! Our eyes are like cameras, they capture almost everything that goes on around us. Some things are meant for our eyes to see and other things aren't. Being on camera can be a little awkward or intimidating sometimes. But once you're comfortable and become more confident being in front of the camera, it becomes natural to you and in a sense you feel free. In other words your life is like an audition. So whatever you do...make sure you do it like no one is watching. That's how you get over the fear of being on camera...just be you! There is a time and place for that of course. :)

GIFT OF APPRECIATION

By Aaron Woodson

Over the years, I've realized something. I've appreciated everything around me except for myself. I've always wanted people to appreciate me, but I've discovered some people have to stumble upon you or wait until you're gone to finally appreciate who you are. The most important thing is to appreciate yourself and what you have instead of what you don't have. The best attitude to have is gratitude. Even though we live life under the sun, we can still live above the sun. Let's face it, everything on this earth is meaningless, you can't take anything you have with you when you're gone. Things depreciate in value over time but people will always remain a treasure! Be kind to one another and appreciate everyone around you. People need to smell their flowers while they are still alive to get them. Thank you all for letting me smell mine while I can still shine! You're wonderful!

LOST AND FOUND

By Aaron Woodson & Jennifer Re

There's no feeling, like it...they said. Love...but no one explains the feeling when it ends. (Jennifer)

"Devastated by its loss, feels like a sad death. Never once thought the love we shared would become a eulogy." (Aaron)

"When did it end? Was there a moment I missed? Was there a look that lingered that Said, 'I can't do this anymore?' (Jennifer)

I wish I knew...things ended between us so prematurely. Our marriage was like our baby...we were expecting a blessing but somehow we had an unfortunate miscarriage! (Aaron)

Pain....my gut was wrenched.

My heart....I needed to forget it existed.

You destroyed me when you left.....but, what I did not know is how to thank you....until today. (Jennifer)

I couldn't pretend any longer and live a lie. I had to leave, it was never the same when you accused me of cheating on you multiple times. You never trusted a word I said except the day we said our vows.
(Aaron)

I'm sorry for the pain and hurt I caused you. I never intended for this to end. (Aaron)
You saw something in them I could never give you
Not even sure I wanted to

But....in trying to please you. In trying to find you I lost me. (Jennifer)

I saw nothing in them...just some random booty calls when you worked late nights or weren't in the mood to give me none. I've always saw something in you...if I didn't, I wouldn't have asked you to be my wife! (Aaron)

I know I cheated and it cut you like a knife. I have to live with regret. I loved you but couldn't be the man you wanted me to be. Now we are separated...the only thing left to do is sign those papers. (Aaron)

But..... I must thank you.
I learned I like eggs....I love them. Scrambled, fried.....
And steaks....I don't like it rare but you do
Avocados suck.....
But cotton candy does not
Puppy kiddies are the best and....
Sex....it is amazing....yes, I like that too

So.... for all the torture and the disgust and the fears you placed there....by losing you, I learned to love me and I'm pretty amazing. For what you took....I forgive you. For what you have me....I thank you.
I have moved.....can you? (Jennifer)

I lost you...but you found yourself. So the outcome has truly left us both LOST & FOUND!

No More Red

By Aaron Woodson

They say we crying over spilled milk, the only thing
we crying over is innocent blood being spilled in these
streets. All I see is red...I know you can see these bull
horns! These mass shootings have been like a game
of bullseye. This isn't a game. Like Jesse Williams,
its time to restructure your function. Like Jada, I ask
why! What's the major malfunction? Ring the alarm...
Code Red Alert. Its time to get in formation. We need
to be unified. We need to work together to solve our
problems. We are a community, but there seems to be
no immunity for senseless violence. Remember our
brains are just as calculating, deadly, and effective as
a gun. Its time to silence the noise of inflammatory
remarks, rhetoric, personal agendas, slander, and gossip!
Let's do something that counts instead of reviewing
the stats of body counts. I know the numbers don't lie
and they are hard to ignore. Like coffee in cream, we
have to rise to the top! We have to make a difference
and take back our streets! Even if we have to protest
to get our point across then so be it! It doesn't matter
what race, origin, ethnicity, religion, gender or political
background you come from...we all matter and we all

bleed red! Enough has been said, let us mourn for our dead and lock arms! No more mental and physical institutions of imprisonment. Its time to remove the shackles and be free! Let's see no more red!

LICENSE TO THRILL

By Aaron Woodson

Incense and Candles...silky smooth grooves invade the air and present a sexy kind of mood! You're presence captivates me, can't help but notice your beautiful curves and seductive lingerie. Got me feelin' some type of way baby, please stop playing with my emotions. You're gonna keep on until I turn the tables on you. Bet you would love that huh? I've got something that you won't know how to handle. I must exercise my authority by showing you I have everything under control. Now sit still and just chill...watch me impose my will. Bend over and take me all inside. We're gonna take it all in stride. Thank you for letting me slip and slide in your playground. I enjoy the sweet sounds of ecstasy you make...it just blows me away like a saxophone. Sharing this moment with you is so euphoric and erotic. Your milky way is so hypnotic and you send nuerotic chills down my spine. Can't believe you're mine! You're fine as wine, you're so divine. You were designed just for me. I'm certified and my credentials speak volumes. I'm licensed to thrill you over and over again...til the next time we meet again!

NEW LEASE

By Aaron Woodson

Out of the depths of debt and adversity came a resurgence if strength and resilience. I faced what seemed like overwhelming odds, yet somehow I overcame and became a pillar. No matter how many times I got knocked down, I kept getting back up! I just couldn't bear yielding myself to defeat, so my determination and faith led me to triumph of these circumstances. In life you make deposits known as costs, everything requires some sort of a cost! It is what it is...I'm just happy to have a new lease on life!

DARK PLACE

By Aaron Woodson

You're like a dark cloud over my head.
There seems to be a storm brewing inside of you that I
haven't been made aware of. I've been waiting patiently
for sunshine to shine through, yet the outlook is still
dim. Tried to lift the conversation higher but I'm not
what you desire. I would like to know what you require.
However, I'm not sure if I'm ready to walk through that
fire. I know what it's like to crash and burn...I gotta let
it burn. Yet again I've turned on the familiar road of
despair. All by myself with no love to share.I've broken
down and I need to be restored. If the angels don't
answer my prayers then whose gonna be there? God
please come find me and meet me where I am. I'm stuck
and I'm in a very dark place. I need to be moved by the
Spirit. I'm waiting for you my LORD, O' God!

QUILT OF LOVE

By Aaron Woodson

God intended for us to be fruitful and multiply. Yet I
see that somewhere in our vast population, that there
is much concentration on the issue of race. As a man
I've faced it...some of you may have encountered it as
well. If we're honest with ourselves we probably all
have experienced it at some point in our lives. But let
me say this my friends, race divides us...it doesn't unite
us. Segregation is a subtraction of a congregation. In
addition, pigmentation of skin has led to a disease
of prejudice, racism, and hate. Allow me to give an
injection of truth to those who are infected. I feel
the need to exercise my poetic justice to a delegation
who fights for civil rights! Freedom and justice for all,
right? Doesn't seem to be the case. Like Snoop once
said, Murder was the case...that's what's happening
in the world today! Everyday there's a homicide...
every day seems like we're told to pick a side. We talk
about violence and gangs, yet this nation is affiliated
with ignorance, hateful slogans, and propaganda. I
come ready with the stanza...it's an extravaganza! In
life you have fans and critics...like Michael Jackson, it
doesn't matter if your black or white. There are more

than 50 shades of grey. Like skittles, I love all colors of the rainbow. If I want to be in a swirlationship, its my prerogative! That's goes for anybody, love sees no color. It knows no barriers...I'm a carrier of love but I'm also a product of it. What difference does it make if we don't look the same? There's nothing wrong at all being different...uniqueness is special and sexy! Its divine and authentic. I'm black as advertised...but I'm more than that! Love defines me, not my skin color! The same goes for you too. I'm a human being just like all of you! Love is the thread and needle that can sew this world back together again! Take off the garment of guilt, and let's wrap ourselves in a quilt of love.

IDENTITY

By Aaron Woodson

People fear what they don't understand. Never should you have to apologize for your existence. We all share time and space...we are all different but all belong to one race...the human race! We are all equal. None more superior or inferior. Love connects us all, it comes from our interior and reflects outside of yourselves. We should never mask our true identity...never forget we are made in the image of God! Doesn't matter what color you are...we all bleed the same color, RED! Character defines you not color...not anything else. Love should be the most important character feature of our identity!

I GOT TO KEEP ON MOVING

By Aaron Woodson

All the stars are aligned...my destiny has already
been designed. Don't need a co-sign...God created
the blueprint and signed off on my greatness! There
is a party going on in heaven...trumpets, drums, and
saxophones are various instruments being played to
commemorate the occassion. I step on the scene and I
take my walk...people watch me as I go by. They have
no idea of the struggle I endured to get here. Behind
every success is struggle...Had to give up to go up. Had
to fall a few times to still be left standing. Nothing ever
was handed to me, I earned what I have at this very
moment. I hate entitlement, most people may share
my sentiment. Passion lit the fuse and an explosion
was imminent. I've blown up and now I'm all grown
up...It's good to see alot of people show up here today.
Funny how I didn't see you during my hard times, but
now you're here for my celebration. You want to take
credit for what you weren't willing to invest. But it's
ok...I made without you! What didn't kill me made me
stronger. Thank you for being here now. So, if you will
excuse me, I got to keep on moving!

PUNCHING BAG

By Aaron Woodson

When I was young child people thought they could
bully me. I was the type that didn't like to fight. Today
is a different story, I'll be ready to throw down because
I don't tolerate bullying of any kind whatsoever! I won't
back down, I'm standing my ground. You don't scare
me. Cowards are not tough to me...you gotta come with
a better tactic. I'm over here getting this money bag.
Keep testing me and I might put you in a body bag. I
used to say I'm a lover not a fighter, but now I say I'm
a lover any anyone can get these holy hands! I train on
the punching bag. I visualize your face on it each time
I hit it! I light up the the bag with these lightening fast
hands...imagine what these hands would do to you. But
I would much rather pray for you. Try messing with the
punching bag before you come see me! The champ has
spoken! Ring the bell...IT'S OVER!

REPARATION

By Aaron Woodson & Aaron Brack

Do you ever ponder, sit and think why?
See in my mind the picture is vivid.
In peace, for peace of mind I just want to leave a legacy
when I die.
The devil is a lie plus the tough times is rigid.
(Aaron B.)

My thoughts are deep as the roots in the soil or you can
even take it further back to my roots of history. I see
how far we have come as a people...we have overcome,
but we still have much further to go in this valley.
The peace of mind we search for can only be found in
the peace of God...the devil has to get behind us, we
know what's in front of us...God will deliver us in His
wonderful timing! (Aaron W.)

Deep in my soul, deep in my roots I smell victory...
Marched as me in unity to transform the evil that
dwells in the air.
See we never had much, only a vivid dream for a future
that is prosperous for me.

Each breathe I take of this polluted air, the powers that Be doesn't play the game fair.

Politics.... hmmm? I have faith that one day this victory for humanity the fight because of plight to exercise my right. A man of dignity, fidelity, and love. (Aaron B.)

A man of vision, purpose, and courage. Together we stand on the front lines of the battlefield conquering our destiny. Putting our lives on the line for the cause. Stop treating our brothers like animals locked in cages. Its so outrageous. Our hearts are wild, no wonder its protected by rib cages. So here we are...the stage has been set for us to be set free! (Aaron W.)

Written on Chrismas Day! 12/25/2017

MUFASA

By Aaron Woodson

We all live under the same sky, but most of us are on different horizons. We all come from the same rock known as planet earth. Since birth, we have all been welcomed to the great circle of life. Most of you have probably seen the film, The Lion King. One the main characters is Mufasa. He was a great and mighty ruler that reigned as the original Lion King. Everything the light touched was his domain. He led and protected his pride. His roar was very powerful. His presence was very commanding and majestic! He also enjoyed a good challenge too. His demeanor was regal, yet fierce. The men in this world can learn and follow the great Mufasa's example of effective leadership. In the face of danger, he was courageous. He demonstrated wisdom and sound judgment. He held those who were under his subjection to the highest accountability. Mufasa was far from passive. He was very poud and intentional. He had a son named Simba that he loved very much. He was very influential to his young son and guided him in the right path of life. Men have a special calling in their lives. Whether we choose to accept it or not, we are looked upon as leaders. We need to be visible, accountable, wise, humble, intentional, courageous, caring, disciplined, protective, proactive, have faith, show love, and be able to provide. Believe it or not, we are someone's Mufasa...someone out there looks up to you. People admire you, they respect you, love you, and may even want to make you proud. Men, it's time to take our rightful place and reign with integrity and leadership. Men, we are lions and we should not be concerned with the opinions of sheep. Live up to your rulership in your respective realms and own your arena! Lions don't live long...however, you can leave a great legacy for future generations in your brief reign. Lions aren't meant to wear muzzles to be silenced. Let everyone hear your roar! Be heard and reject passivity! Men be who you are...don't be afraid of who you are or what you'll be become. If you're a father, be FATHER! If you're a leader, be a LEADER! If you're a husband, be a HUSBAND! You're a male by birth, but you have to earn the right to call yourself a man! If you're man... damn it, BE A MAN! You're a king...Hakuna Ma-ta-ta! Means no worries. You're a champion! ROAR with pride. Don't hide in the shadows...step out in faith and be the Mufasa I know we all can be!

HERE'S THE THING

By Aaron Woodson

Here's the thing...some people who are together are not even in a relationship. They are a thing with nothing that defines their relationship status. Its like a half-hearted agreement made by two people just going through the motions. Its more of a casual fling rather than a full blown committment. The purpose isn't intentional which makes it pretty delusional. It's complicated, yet confusing. Friends with benefits with no strings attached may be the motto...but neither one of them has exactly hit the lottery of love. Chances are slim to none for that to ever happen. Those people have an agreement for this unique arrangement known as a flirtationship. They play by their own set of rules... if only they had a clue of what true love really is! That's the thing.

THE HEART OF A POET

By Aaron Woodson

Where ever you are. What ever you're doing. Just
know I'm thinking of you. Miles may separate us but
our bond will always remain strong and close. Sweet
memories will survive...love never dies, it just thrives! I
never knew what love really was until I met you. You're
beautiful presence is what I look forward to. Baby, I
miss your essence. I've always adored you. I wish you
were here...if only time stayed still for just a little bit
longer. The absence has made my heart grow fonder. No
wonder I'm over here going crazy! I hope you're feeling
the same way about me too. I always I enjoyed hearing
you speak my name. The sound of your voice lifted
me a little higher. Whatever fire that burned inside of
me, you fueled it with so much desire! Love is all I ever
required. How sweet it is to be loved by you. I love you
more than you'll ever know. Let's grow old and hold
each other like we never wanna let go! I don't mind
having you around. You truly make my heart sing baby!
I Thank God for you everyday! Know my heart...a heart
is in the house tonight! Let me know if you heard my
heartbeat! Its the Heart of A Poet!

CRAZY, SEXY, COOL

By Aaron Woodson (Dedicated to TLC)

A legendary trio that made us wanna creep. They took us way back and made us wanna kick a little game. We all know them as TLC...Crazy, Sexy, Cool. They inspired a young generation with their feminine anthems, party jams, and a style that was ahead of their time. I remember listening to their jams on a Sunday afternoon, I just didn't care who was there! Whenever I was in the mood for some good lovin'...The Red Light Special would really turn me on. I'm definately no scrub and know my way around these parts. Never was too proud to beg when I needed some the most. Used to chase waterfalls and now I'm staying the course. All that I've been through and still go through...I know I can still be Crazy, Sexy, Cool!

SOCIAL MEDIA

By Aaron Woodson

The world is rapidly changing with this phenomenon
we call social media. So what exactly is social media?
It's defined as websites and applications that enable
users to create and share content or to participate in
social networking. Social media is very interactive
and highly engaging to a worldwide audience. We are
connected through an online community. So much
content is broadcast on social media platforms. People
create accounts and profiles to social media websites
such as Facebook, Facebook Messenger, Instagram,
Snapchat, WhatsApp, Twitter, YouTube, and more.
It doesn't take long for something that is posted to go
viral in a matter of seconds. Social media can often lead
people to a downward spiral. Some concerns of the use
of social media is verbal abuse, bullying, harassment,
and trolling. Social Media can unfairly judge, criticize,
label, slander and give false perceptions of people. Social
media can be a distraction and can often be a waste of
time. There are benefits to social media and the major
purpose for it is simply communication! Society use
to rely on traditional media and journalism outlets...
now times have changed. We are in the Digital Age

and so many of us including myself are caught up in its deception. Social media can be a form of manipulation and can exploit others at their own expense. Social media has become influential and helpful in many ways. However, on the other side of the coin it can be a tool of destruction. Social media is like a disease, we can become infected if we aren't careful. We can become an addict to social media. The powers that be that are pulling the strings are secretly controlling us by way of social media. Be warned...sometimes you need to log out of the system and check into real life. The life that we are living in this very moment...

LOVE YOUR NEIGHBOR

By Aaron Woodson

I've accepted that some people love me. Some dislike
me. Some respect me. And some could care less. I'm
the same way. The beautiful thing about life is choice...
people make their own choices! We live in a world
where phones are given more attention than individual
people. Communication seems to be too much to ask
for these days. I understand people get busy including
myself...making time for someone can be challenging
this day in age. Most people have so many things to do.
There are priorities we must arrange in our daily lives.
Problems are something we all have in common and
sometimes can just be unavoidable. When problems are
arise, some people tend to become reclusive and become
introverted. Circumstances will test you and its possible
for to grow through them. Excuses, disappointments,
fear, and setbacks can prevent progression which is
known as regression. It's not about what happens to
you. It's about what happens through you. People are
meant to share a connection with each other. Caring
and loving is the theme. Everyone is valuable and are
a gift to the world. Treat others like you want to be

treated. People are not things...we all mean something. If not we would never have been created to exist! We all live in the same space...we don't own anything. Love your neighbor!

BEAUTY AND THE BEAST

By Aaron Wooodson

A fairy tale arises as it becomes a reality from the imagination! I am the narrarator and character of a love story that comes to life which is called Beauty and the Beast! In the midst of a storm, The Beast dwells in the walls of his dark gloomy castle like a prisoner from the outside world. He isolated, lonely, confused, and in a constant rage! He observes life from the window of his fortress. He hides the man that he truly is and hope his destiny will bring him his true love! Could it be that I'm the beast? Maybe so or am I just fearful to love's heartache? Does my cry for beauty fall upon deaf ears? Wherever you are...whoever you are, please answer my call fair beauty!

On the Ropes

By Aaron Woodson

As I stand in love's presence, I marvel at its amazing power! I'm touched deeply by this mighty force, it causes me tremble with passion. I have no choice but to cave in from the pressure, now I'm buried underneath all this treasure. I remember there were times I wasn't very embracing to love. Somehow, I would look for the nearest exit and abandon ship! I was thrown a line and to my surprise, love had come to my rescue. I could have drowned from all of my fears, tears, and pain...yet by some divine intervention I made it back to shore. Despite all I've been through, love had melted through my defenses and made me come to my senses! I used to think of love as my sparring partner...we'd put on our gloves and hit each other with our best shot. I guess you could say love got the better of me during the exchange. I was knocked down a few times, dizzy, and even wobbly against the ropes at times. Through it all, I stood tall and if it weren't for love...I'd certainly be laid out on the canvas! My opponent had me against the ropes, but

I absorbed the punishment. I fought back and talked smack. I was

THE MEANING OF CHRISTMAS

By Aaron Woodson

Christmas is absolutely the most commercialized holiday of the year. Christmas can be the most wonderful time of the year for most people. For the rest of us it could be the most depressing time of the year. Christmas is in the winter season and the weather is usually pretty cold. There are many homeless left out in the streets with no shelter. People are often lonely and miserable during the holidays. Some of us may have lost loved ones or you could be reminded of the void that was left. Sometimes people lose their jobs during this time of year. The struggle to pay bills and buy Christmas gifts can be a hard decision. Stress is at an all-time high during the Christmas season. Long lines in the local stores and traffic jams along the roads can be irritating for most of us. I would like to believe that the meaning of Christmas is more than our circumstances and what is advertised. Christmas is about giving, caring, and sharing. It's about love, kindness, goodness, and gathering together. The cornerstone of Christmas is about the birth of our Savior, Jesus Christ! Nativity took place and the world can be naive to what actually occurred. The true meaning of Christmas is the arrival of the Messiah, Jesus Christ!

DESERVE MORE

By Aaron Woodson

Open your eyes. Make up your mind. Tell me what version you prefer or maybe you prefer replacement. You've become complacent here lately. Are you aware that complacency kills? Our relationship is suffering and it's dying before we know it. Please don't blow it. I won't even show it. Out that door I'll go and never come back. I deserve so much better. I deserve more!

REJUVENATED

By Aaron Woodson

Our love is beyond description couldn't skip this any
better Faith passion and dedication is are recommended
prescription the remedy for deception is speaking
R-Truth confusion is a misconception wisdom is the
Divine conception. Half the population suffer for lack
of knowledge five languages of love which do you speak
five senses to help us survive in this habitat there is a
realm of possibilities just need to find one solution no
more salt in the wound stop covering up with a Band-
Aid there is nothing more powerful than healing God
is the master of this practice he taught it to his disciples
he's got more followers than your Facebook Instagram
or SnapChat reach for the stars and read the caption I
am the creator of this universe I made you in my image
you were made with love and you have a hope and a
future reading obey my scriptures. Only then you will
have been rejuvenated.

KICK AND PUSH

By Aaron Woodson & Amalia Grattieri

I see you sitting there looking so beautiful with such a radiant glow. Its a phenomenal accomplishment to see us going half on a baby... (Aaron Woodson)

Half of our genes. Intertwined like our souls, manifested into this beautiful being that will be of our making. Love is the glow that exudes from my pores. This baby mine and yours. Blessed is an understatement of what is to occur. (Amalia G.)

A bond so strong...no wonder we can't resist being so fond of one other. My heart pulsates with great anticipation. The love we share is so euphoric. A divine chemistry that was born led to the perfect experiment of our beautiful unborn seed. (Aaron Woodson)

To be born of our flesh, with so much possibility. A perfect blend of you and me. I never believed a love like this could exist but now I feel it when I think of this blessing. Beautiful, uncertain and everything I ever wished it could be. (Amalia G.)

We mesh together like yin and yang. Our baby brings so much love and joy. The arrival of this wonderful blessing was right on schedule. Your womb held our little mystery...now we have unlocked a beautiful secret. An angel has been revealed. A new chapter awaits all three of us...it's a dream come true. And to think it all started with a kick and push! (Aaron Woodson)

GREATEST OF ALL TIME

By Aaron Woodson

When I think about this special person I see a Pioneer
that leaves behind a legacy that no other can match
she is the most devoted loyal loving courageous and
powerful woman I've ever known ladies and gentlemen
she is my grandmother Miss Fannie Mae Wallace
throughout her life time she has taken on many titles
but only one can surely do her justice she has the
greatest of all time in many ways she was like the
general of our family that let us through every battle
with great wisdom her marching orders were always
carried out and we dare not a poser I remember my
father wasn't around and she told me God knows what
he did and he will keep encounter what he did to you
forgive him he is still your father! She always put things
in such a way that I could understand I always looked
up to her and she was the rock that I ran to whenever
I was in trouble. Granny was a name me and your
other grandkids would call you because we just loved
and adored you so you spoiled Us Rotten at times but
you chastised us when we got out of line you took me
everywhere you went and taught me how to be the man
I am today I've seen you go through so much but you
always manage to tough it out on the battlefield I am a
soldier and I salute the greatest of all time.

BIG PAPA

By Aaron Woodson

Like the season Redwood that stands taller than any
other tree Big Poppa you always were strong never did
you go down when others try to chop you down you
stuck to your roots and you are deeply Center to Earth
Big Poppa you were Larger than Life everyone looked
up to you and each time you are soft for wisdom your
shape protected all who stood by you big poppa you
always were proud and a mighty force to be reckoned
with! Thank you for the love you display to help me
grow into the man I am today! Your spirit will live
on Big Poppa and for now I realize you must rest Big
Poppa you truly were the best and no one can ever
can test your greatness there isn't enough words in the
dictionary that can divide Define what Big Poppa stats
for Big Poppa you made the world go around as you
ascend into heaven ask God if he can give you one more
chance because I would like to dance with my father
again.

FACE THE MUSIC

By Aaron Woodson

Turn the music up now I got to hear that beat drop
s*** hits hard 808 blaring got these haters glaring got
the lady staring All Eyez on Me Like infrared Beams I
got to take one for the team I can't pretend that I didn't
offend trying to make amends for my wrongs like Jay-Z
I can make this song cry so I'll do my best impression
like Usher these are my confessions I'm not scared but
I do go to church I did my dirt and yes I know I hurt
you. My actions were inappropriate s****** gone wrong
wish I could take it all back I got nothing but love
for you but secretly I wouldn't mind giving you that
vitamin D. Milk sure does a body good but I'd rather
have your Sunny Delight all jokes aside my pride is
on the line I'm a man that f***** up I ask you straight
to your face to forgive me will make it through this
episode don't have to pull out the violins yet just need
time to heal you want to keep your distance I respect
your stance I salute you hope I didn't lose one but if I do
sometimes you got to lose some to win some I'm sorry
I'm a champion although I feel the percussion of the
repercussion I Know I can face the music!

CHECK YOUR INBOX

By Aaron Woodson

Poetry is my text I'm the sender and I'm just waiting for your reply I hope you receive a blessing from the words a man speaks from his heart do your part and be my sweetheart you got the four-one-one so it's up to you to make an intelligent decision feel free to leave a voicemail at your discretion because hearing from you brings excitement like an erection you feel me haha I always do it big like notorious so if you're curious then baby give me one more chance.

WORTH THE WAIT

By Aaron Woodson

It would be a dream come true if I could find a special one to be on my team. Together her and I could be All-Stars! All my life actually got it for my potential lover but I have yet to find her I thought maybe I'd cross paths with her along this journey maybe I'm lost I probably am blind to see who she really is the future seems foggy waiting for the forecast to clear up or I could just walk by faith and wait on God I'll be patient because I know my true love will be worth the wait.

Departure and Arrival

By Aaron Woodson

Life without you seems like a catastrophe like a word
that is incomplete I'm missing my apostrophe our
story began and they came to an end before we had a
chance to grow as one you leaving me feels like a defeat
but I realize you just retreated back into your comfort
zone I'm concentrating on being alone and accepting
this miserable out come I can honestly say that I was
considerably in love with you. Reminiscing about
the intimate and private Rendezvous we used to have
with one another oh how sweet were those encounters
eventually I had to take everything with a grain of
sugar that turned into salt yes I admit I've tasted been
to this but now I'm drinking out of a new cup filled
with fresh lemonade had to turn these lemons into
something right there is a saying that goes out of sight
out of mind but what's funny is that even though you're
out of sight I still can't seem to get you out of my mind
I will find my escape and make a new landscape I shall
reap a new Harvest and sit back and enjoy a glass of
wine from a field of grapes the memories will always be
there except you won't be in my next chapter after the
rain there will be sunshine my sunshine will embrace

me with her beautiful rays of joy and warmth I will soak up all of her love and I will be illuminated with her amazing Radiance together we will experience a new ambient romance and new alluring fragrance of Happiness to last lifetime these are the sign of the times the beginning of a new era there has been a departure and I'm expecting an arrival here very soon!

DEAR GOD

By Aaron Woodson

Dear God it's your servant and child Aaron I come
before you to lay my burdens and transgressions at your
feet Lord you know I fall short daily I'm not worthy
I'm just a man you have all the power your omnipresent
you're everything I could never be I am in awe of you.
Lord you brought me into this world and I'm not so
sure why sometimes I feel as if I disappointed you I
often feel as if I've falling way behind. I sometimes feel
as though you don't hear my prayers but I know that
isn't true because you loved me you know my heart and
what I'm most desire however I also know what you
require you want obedience prayer reading your word
and doing good to others to be honest I have struggled
doing all of that and I'm working to do better in those
areas of my life I know I am blessed I don't want to
seem selfish or anything, but I really would like to have
a wife I believe that would be a welcomed addition to
my life I need a help mate and a virtuous woman who
will love me and be a blessing to me I understand that
all things come to those who wait I've been waiting a
long time and seeing other people being so happy there
are other times I feel as though I'm overlooked I don't

feel as though I'm entitled but it says in your word to ask seek and it shall be given to you I also realized that I need to seek you first in the kingdom of God and all those things shall be added unto me I am seeking you Lord what is your plan for me you told me that you would give me a hope and a future I know that you are not a god of confusion you are a God of vision.

ARMY OF GOD

By Aaron Woodson

Christian Soldier report all present and accounted
for sir fall in line Soldier... Enlisted Army of God
forward March! We are Gods infantry and we are on
the battlefield for our Lord. We have an enemy that we
can't identify, but we know it's Satan and his demons.
Prepare for spiritual warfare and put on the whole
armor of God. When God is for us who can be against
us. We've got the Victory and will strike a mighty blow
into this ministry of evil and bring them to their knees!
Every knee must bow and every tongue must confess
that he is Lord. Clench your swords for the battle is
the Lord's and let his word make Satan and his army
flinch! The smell of fear is in the air and the hunters
have just become the hunted. The Holy Spirit prevails
over the flesh. The regime of evil will be put to an end
by The Sovereign supreme God once and for all. Many
are called but few are chosen. We have been chosen as
God's people to serve the only true Living God. We
are the army of God, here we stand and serve God
Almighty always and forever...Amen!

Every Man 4 Himself

By Aaron Woodson

You and I have been the best of friends...we both share a strong camaraderie like brothers in arms. Never have we double-crossed or caused one another any harm. This very moment can change all of that. There is a common denominator that affects us and perhaps it will make or break this friendship. Some things can be shared with others while other things can't. Many places you can go with someone but there are times you have to go it alone. Sometimes you just know there will be someone out there you have to contend with. That very person maybe someone close to you like your best friend. We are both romantically linked to a special girl. Problem is we both can't have her...only one of us will have a chance. It's every man for himself. Will one of us survive? What happens thereafter? The outcome will decide the fate of who wins or who goes home. At the end of the day we're still going to be boys no matter what please believe that.

FLYING HIGH

By Aaron Woodson

It's a bird...it's a plane...it's the U.S. Air Force soaring
through the unfriendly and enduring freedom skies!
Just when you thought the battle was done and yet
the war has just begun. And to think all it took was a
heinous, psychotic, and unthinkable act of evil to bring
down two mighty towers into rubble on American soil.
The date is known and never will be forgotten. The
result was shock and terror, disbelief, and confusion!
Throughout the tragedy of chaos we as a nation
ask "Why?" Mystery surrounds a never before seen
controversy and yet no answers have been disclosed
we the United States of America. We demand respect,
retribution, and justice. Those that have opposed us
have made a very fatal mistake because we are a force
to be reckoned with. No one else comes close and now
your time has come to meet your doom. Brace yourself,
for this will be the last day of light you'll ever see again.
We take no prisoners, we just take you out just like that!
Ready to rock and roll...ready to take control! Ready to
kick some ass. Let's do it and get the job done. We're
flying High. Who are we? The United States Air Force...
Mighty, mighty Air Force!

"WOULD YOU..."

By Aaron Woodson

Baby I can't help but wonder... so I was hoping that maybe you could help me out! Are you all that you say you are or is it just pretend? Whatever your intentions maybe I will still love you no matter what! I ask nothing more in return except...

"Would you be my one and only?"
"Would you be there for me in my time of need?"
"Would you ever change the way you feel about me?"
"Would you ever walk away from me?" "Would you ever love me?" "Would you ever look at me the same or differently?" "Would you ever take me seriously or as a joke?" "Would you ever accept me for the way I am?" "Would you make me better?" "Would you ever lie to me?" "Would you ever cry for me?" "Would you die for me?" "Would you keep it real?" "Would you be the woman I know and love?" "Would you be understanding?" "Would you judge me?" "Would you even care?" "Would you hold me close?" "Would you ever kiss me goodbye?" "Would you embrace me like the morning sunshine?" "Would you ever show your true colors?" "Would you ever miss me if I were gone?"

I don't know what the future holds, so day by day I live for us to someday be together! Only time will tell...I know what I would do right now. It's your move, I just wish u would.

Someday

By Aaron Woodson

Someday you and I will meet face-to-face. Someday our eyes will undress each other in public and behind closed doors. Someday our hands will touch and make contact. Those same hands are anxious to circulate and navigate each other's physical being. Someday the hands of time will remind us that our time has come. Someday our lives will be more meaningful than ever before. Someday our love will bloom like a rose which means we will open up to each other and live happily under the sun. Someday we will have to endure the rain. Someday we will weather the storm. Someday our passion and affection will give us comfort and protection. Someday we will grow with unity and strength. Someday we will experience our first kiss. Someday we will experience real love through our intensity desire and faith. Someday you and I will start a family of our own. Someday we will grow old together through periods of time. Someday you and I will experience the last kiss. With knowing all of this will be together always someday.

WELCOME TO A BETTER PLACE

By Aaron Woodson

All I can think of is how much of a special person you
were and forever continue to be. Nothing will ever
overshadow the kind of loving person I've known and
grown to love. You are a gift sent from heaven up above.
You gave us a sweet taste of who you truly are and
always will be. For now, we realize that you are gone
but you will always remain in our hearts. The way you
were taken from us was very heartbreaking and painful
to all of us. So now you have gained your wings and
ascended up to heaven smiling down on those who
loved you. Although, most of us didn't get a chance
to say goodbye...we know that you're in a better place!
From us to you...welcome to a better place and we hope
to make it there with you someday.

SPEED BUMPS

By Aaron Woodson

I'm riding in my Chevy, rolling through the hood. the
pavement is hot and heavy. Music turnt all the way
up, blasting out the trunk. Bobbin' to the sound of my
poetic flow, straight got that Uptown Funk like Bruno
Mars. Tryna ride slow and enjoy my day Chopped and
Screwed. Life got me all twisted...some of y'all got me
all dusted n disgusted. Ugly girls vying for my attention,
I'll keep my foot on the gas and go past them speed
bumps. Sometimes you got to take your lumps, but I
ain't no chump...now I'm pumpin' these brakes when I
see a fine girl come by my way. I want her to back it up
on me like a dump truck. She got me kind of stuck on
a feeling. Daydreaming about putting her up against
my wall I make her reach for the ceiling with the high
notes I'll be havin' her singin'. It's been a bumpy road.
I hit everything with full force. Navigating through
these issues, sometimes I'm left drifting. Life makes you
shift gears and you just have to come off the clutch and
accelerate. Lived life in the fast lane, looking through
my rearview all I can remember is bittersweet memories
and windowpane. I put a lot of miles on this trip and
I'm still driving to my final destination. So many things

to see and so many Honey-do's! Pardon me, I would rather have my ride or die chick go along with me and say, "I Do." Together we would be a match made in heaven...a formidable duo and team! Been through too many speed bumps, maybe there's a smoother road to get to my trophy. Winning my baby's heart would be better than winning the Daytona 500. Until then I will continue to run my race. Please remember my handsome face, I was meant to be seen on the billboard. Cameras flashing, I'm ready for this moment. I have no speed bumps that appear on the surface. I'm in the clear like Cleared. Push it to the Limit and watch out for those speed bumps!

I Do

By Aaron Woodson

Sweetheart, there isn't anyone I would possibly say or do this for except you. Please take this time to relax your mind and open up your heart. Let my words sooth you like a quiet storm as the rain pours. My love for you seeps down like a waterfall. Before I say no over yes, I want you to know it will always be yes over and over for you. There isn't anything I wouldn't do for you. Let it be known baby... I do want you I do need you. I do think about you. I do dream about you. I do miss you. I do cherish you. I do it for me and you. I do it for here now and forever. I do love you and most of all I do want to spend the rest of my glorious days with you. Be mine and I'll be yours. Do it for me and I'll do more. That I do promise you because you mean everything to me.

THE SCENE

By Aaron Woodson

Quiet on the set a production is taking place by my
direction and expertise. I'm the writer, composer,
executive producer, manager, director, and actor. This
feature captures every angle position and performance
of our presentation. It's more than just a spectacle
of our imagination because this is for real! Nothing
Hollywood or Broadway...just a masterpiece that grabs
the attention of viewers in their own privacy! This
demonstration what we call the scene seems very up-
close-and-personal! There are no retakes, but if we make
just the right adjustments we will perfectly execute
our roles! The roles that you and I play in this scene
is the intimate passion of foreplay which is a form of
love! Creativeness, and over emphasism is the key to
this work of art! The time has come for us to perform
the scene, so now we can enjoy the show! Seduction
is beginning to set in and now the action is getting
started! Clothes are removed and fall to the floor...then
our lips touch as our tongues begin to tangle! With
every gentle stroke, we caress one another into sweet
ecstasy. Sounds of relief and affection take over the air.
It echoes into full effect! And now to be continued...

we will do the rest of the scene privately behind closed doors. Stay tuned and rehearse your own scene because the scene of our love is remarkably the best. Nothing else can ever compare.

WHERE

By Aaron Woodson

The setting takes place where..."where is where?" Who
knows? All I know is where my loved dwells and that
is in my heart! Where is the destination unknown and
it leads to wherever the distance may go! Where can
be near or far and maybe even all around! Could it be
my love is targeting you or is it that I myself could be a
target? Where is the bullseye on the target? Where does
love point to? Where is like a buried treasure but it can
be found! Where can be a position but baby please tell
me what your favorite position? Where does it start?
Where does it end where do we draw the line? Like a
puzzle, pieces of the answers are still missing...where
to find them remains to be seen! Where is the presence
of yesterday, today, and tomorrow! Where exists and
revolves around location, but yet will we ever take the
time to find it?And when we do find it where will it be?
Where we all go is up to us and it's our choice on where
it is we go!

WHY

By Aaron Woodson

Why this...why that why ask why? Or maybe should I not ask why. The very utterance of why is all around like a faint whisper in the air! A word that is often spoken in our curiosity, confusion, disbelief, and amazement to such effects. Why pleads for an explanation and sometimes there is one or there isn't. Why is not the solution to every problem, instead it is a learning process! We learn why things happen the way they happen! We learn why things are the way they truly are! And sometimes we learn why we do the things that we do! Whether or not we choose to accept why...well that is simply up to us! Why ask why? Maybe so that we can understand or comprehend, but whatever the case maybe... why is like an unsolved mystery waiting to be discovered. You never know unless you know why!

Cut It

By Aaron Woodson

I'm Cut From a different cloth...my style is one-of-a-kind. I'm a rare breed, a lone wolf that had to separate from the rest of the pack. Life didn't cut me any slack, so don't give me any flack for living the way that I do. From birth, the cord had to be cut. My mother and father nurtured me with love. But I learned to grow independently. I remember trying out for the high school basketball team it didn't make the cut. Of course I was disappointed and thought I wasn't cut out for anything. Like Aaliyah, I had to dust myself off and try again. I'll never forget my classmate's life was cut much too short...it was Murder She Wrote, that s*** cut so deep. I guess life's tragedy is a familiar scene, lights camera action! Then all of a sudden it's a wrap... CUT! There's a long line outside the club to get in, ladies always trying to cut in front of you. I don't mind at all, besides I get to watch them wear their sexy Daisy Duke cut-off shorts. Skirts and low-cut tops are really my weakness. Oh my God! They really need to cut it out right now. Thinking about my approach, I need to use caution before I proceed to one of them. Can't stop thinking about peaches and cream...so I decide to make my move. I cut right to the chase I told her she was cut like a diamond and above all the rest. Heart pounding in my chest, breaking a cold sweat. Just trying to be sure. She's so pure. Waiting for her reaction. She smiles and cuts me off gently saying she has a boyfriend. I understood and walked away yet again disappointed. A long drive home is what I look forward to at the end of the night. But not so fast, I witness an accident on the side of the road. Apparently someone cut another person off on the intersection. I wish people had a better sense of direction. That night I got home and thought about the accident I just witnessed. It reminded me of my wreck years ago. Thank God I lived through it and didn't need any surgery. Well it's time for me to go to sleep. I got plans to get my haircut at the barbershop, cut the grass, and take a shortcut to the mall. I always enjoy the end of the year cut off prices. Have to get my scissors out and cut out my coupons...gotta use them before it's too late! The cut off is January 1st. It's a New Year... I'm going to be quick to cut people off especially fake friends. My circle way too big, I need to cut it. Cut it...Cut it...Cut it!!!

Poetic Justice Meets Love Jones

(Dedicated to Janet Jackson)

Legendary. Sexy. Brilliant. Revolutionary. Iconic.
Powerful. Brave. Stunning. Ladies and gentlemen, she
is the one and only Queen of Pop Janet Jackson!!! Her
smile radiates like the shining sun and brings me so
much joy. She commands attention and her powerful
presence captivates and mesmerizes you! There are
times when I look above and beyond. There are times
when I feel her love around me. I can never forget my
baby Janet Jackson! Always been an inspiration and
true angel to me. I always dreamed about seeing her
dancing in moonlight. If she was my girl I could just
imagine all the things she'd do to me. I definitely would
call out her name. She taught me through her music
that it doesn't really matter what the eye is seeing. Cuz
I'm in love with the inner being. And it doesn't matter
what they believe, what matters to me is that she's in
love with me. She's what I asked for. She's so loving
and kind and I can't believe I got to see her in concert.
I wish she was all mine! One day, I hope to finally find
somebody whose heart is true and best of all that she's

nutty-nutty-nutty for me. I would love to take her on an Escapade and just hear her feedback! When I think of her, I wonder how funny time flies when we're having fun. Sometimes I get so lonely, can't let just anybody hold me. She is the one that lives in me, my dear. Want no one but her! All my life I've waited to see Janet smile again. In my mind I hated that her show was cancelled. One day she decided to come back to me on her State of The World Tour. Lord knows I've tried to live my life as one. Friends told me to hold on. Tough times don't last for long. My abandoned heart just never understood. My undying love for her wouldn't let me wait. Thank God you came back to me. I missed you much. I really missed you much! All I want to say is Anytime, Anyplace. I don't care who's around! Miss Jackson you know I'm nasty, but you're in control. Maybe we can take it slow...let's wait awhile or we might take it too far. We ain't going to ever get no sleep. Someday we'll be together again. Poetic Justice meets Love Jones. A bond that will forever be inseparable...it's unshakable... it's UNBREAKABLE!

NEVER AGAIN

By Aaron Woodson

You want me to remember your name, but fail to
remember mine. You expect me to be this and that or
have it all, yet you don't have it all together either. You
never ask how my day is. You don't even put forth the
effort. I guess I'll remain invisible to you. I always let
my light shine but you're too blind to see. You want
everyone and everything else but me you're just not
that interested that I can truly see. Guess we were never
meant to be. I'm just a fly on the wall to you. I'm much
more than you think I am. You're just lost in the sauce.
I'm a boss and I'm flyer than a kite. I soar like an eagle...
watch me take flight. Don't worry I'll be out of your
sight. Watch me become a household name, I'll be a
dream come true to my number one fan. Never again!

SPIDER-MAN

By Aaron Woodson

I'm going to need you to fall back, now lay down on your back...cuz that's where I want you! Don't move, shh...don't say a word. I crawl on you like a spider and got you tangled up in my web of love. Things are about to get sticky tonight. I'm the hunter and you're my prey. Don't fight it, let me have my way. Feel my sting of passion as I penetrate deep inside. I got you paralyzed with ecstacy and now you're under my control. Each thrust is delivered with such power and precision. Feel my extension as we release these tensions. Your body speaks to me like a foreign language. I study it diligently to make myself that much more fluent. I see your face buried in the pillow, tell me...what are you saying to it? I see you're getting all into it. Yeah baby that's right you know how I do! Hearing you yell and say my name is music to my ears! Making love to you is just pure bliss and brings tears to my eyes. All my fears and insecurities have vanished like the wind. Since you came into my life. I don't have eight legs but I'm a freak. That's the language I speak. There are many different dialects of it, hopefully you enjoyed the curriculum.

I'm the web slinger...The Amazing Spider-Man! I always stay fly and I need you to be my Mary Jane. I'll always be there for you sincerely your friendly superhero Spider-Man.

REVIVED

By Aaron Woodson

I can't hide my pride, so much that I hold deep inside. This life has been a rollercoaster ride of ups and downs. I've been living on the edge. I'm on the verge of falling off my cliff. I've tried to escape these crazy thoughts going on inside my mind. You can only outrun them for so long until they finally catch up to you. I've learned you just have to let it happen. When you survive the worst part, you can breathe and say you made it. Bittersweet Memories always seemed to linger. I just can't put my finger on why they still remain. I attempt to find therapy and meaningless activity but it's only a temporary relief from the torture. I have a hard time living with myself. The fear of dying alone scares the hell out of me. These dark secrets I swore I'd never tell. I've always lived by the code of confidentiality. Until I realized that you can hide from people but you can't hide from God. He knows me from the inside out. Prayer has been my greatest therapy and God has been my Wonderful Counselor. He understands me even when people misunderstand me. He even understands me when I don't quite understand myself at times. I've lived in pain, shame, and resentment for too long... It's time to break out of this yoke of bondage. Every Chain must be broken by the anointing. The past isn't meant to haunt, its meant to teach! I was directed by the Holy Spirit and it guided me through uncertainty. My steps were ordered while in the desert. God has carried me through the worst and best of times. All is well within my soul. I am clothed with joy and I am dancing because I have the victory. I celebrate having a new life and purpose in Christ. I am revived!

Onion

By Aaron Woodson

Excuse Me miss, why are you crying? As she's choking on her words between sobs, I noticed that she's cutting an onion. I kind of look at her like "Wow, this onion really got her all emotional. That's it! I begin to realize that she represents the onion and if you want to reach the center you got to peel her back one layer at a time. All these layers are just protective covers to shield the pain that she may be experiencing on the surface. She looks so beautiful, but at her core she is vulnerable. Pain runs deep, she hardly gets any sleep. The odor of the onion that she's cutting is torturing my sinuses. Her fragrance is the opposite, it's very sweet and alluring. When I look behind her, I'm happy to notice that she has an onion booty. It literally can make a grown man cry. Lord have mercy! As a man I have to comfort her and maybe ask her out for lunch. I'm thinking we can have some onion rings and enjoy a nice conversation. This onion philosophy is really intriguing to me...besides I've got some onion dip she might want to try.

Take Charge

By Aaron Woodson

I was born a boy yet I grew into a man like a toddler
trying to take his first steps I fell a few times. That
didn't stop me from being determined to walk mistakes
I've made became lessons some things were self-taught
and other things I learned from mentors. I also learn
from other people's mistakes too that's the beauty of
Being Human no matter how I'm perfect we are we
still strive to get it right in life. I could sing songs for
all the wrongs I've done but I can't leave out the high
notes that will carry on for as long as I live for me
being a man is mandatory there's just no other way
around it. A man shouldn't be defined by a stature he
should be defined by his posture and maturity and
man shouldn't be defined by how much money he has
he should be defined by all the live he helps to enrich.
A man shouldn't be defined by the shackles of his
past he should be defined by what he has overcome
by his testimony and man shouldn't be defined by its
popularity a man should be defined by how he uplift
others real men get down on their knees and pray. Real
men don't abuse others using their masculinity real
men aren't arrogant or prideful they are humble real

men praise the name of Jesus Kingdom men about their father's business. Men have to renew their minds daily man it's time for us to love lead and defend courageously every move we make should be intentional and positively Proactive man we need to surround ourselves with a Band of Brothers sometimes in life we can find ourselves thinking but remember God is our anchor. Are lifeguard walks on water we should never take our eyes off of him also men we have to remember in order to move forward we must break every chain that keeps us bound we are not captive we are free forgive those who know not what they do. Show mercy and Grace to others because our father has given the same to you man leave behind excuses and just do what you're called to do be a man act like a man Think Like a Man believe in yourselves men! However trust in God and lean not on your own understanding God loves you man he made you in His image he had all of you in mind and he created everything for you stand up and live Godly live you're from this world but you're not of this world you are a Godly Man and that is your identity walk in the truth be the light and bring it everywhere you go. take charge men!

PEP TALK

By Aaron Woodson

Everyone has choices but sometimes we get influenced by other voices. Seems like doing what is right is the hardest thing for most of us to do. We often choose what we know to be wrong because it feels good or it is a better alternative to doing what's right. People talk about freedom and how they have a right to be entitled to something, yet they won't fight for their rights and believe they are free to receive. What they don't realize is that everything in life has a cost. What are you willing to sacrifice? What are you willing to go through to become successful? Everyone wants to feel loved and be loved... however, you must give love to receive love. Everything in life is about give and take. It's true we all make mistakes but the beauty of it is that we can all learn the lessons we've been taught. If you want to inspire change in our broken world we must be willing to change who we are and get involved! The world is full of problems, yet we can solve many of them by putting our best foot forward to make a difference. The world doesn't revolve around us, we are not orbiters. Gravity keeps us on solid ground. And we experience the great circle of life. Like the sun, we rise and fall. Everything is in a delicate balance. We become one with our universe and we should give praise to the creator of the universe. Amen.